Beyond Survival

(Revitalizing the Small Church)

By

James E. Cushman

Published by The Evangelism and
Church Development Ministry Unit
Presbyterian Church (U.S.A.)
Louisville, Kentucky

Standard Book Number 87012–391–2
Library of Congress Card Number 80–84345
Printed in the United States of America
Copyright © 1981 by James E. Cushman
Ripley, West Virginia
All Rights Reserved

Second printing, 1990

This book is dedicated to the members of the Beverly Presbyterian Church. The love and care of the members of this congregation for one another and for our family has been a living demonstration of the unique nature of the small church. The experience of working with this faithful group of Christians as they have worked together to revitalize their congregation has served as the real inspiration for this book.

In addition, the book is dedicated to the Presbytery of Greenbrier, and particularly to Al Cowan, Executive Presbyter, and the other Presbytery staff members. The experience of working with judicatory leaders who are seriously trying to create a presbytery that supports and helps the small church has indeed been an exciting adventure.

Table of Contents

v

CHAPTER ONE

The Small Church Today

The Small Church as a Problem

The small church is a problem. Ask any denominational executive and you will discover that to be true. The small church is a problem. Why?

First, almost all small churches are unsuccessful. In success oriented American society, small churches do not measure up to any of the standards of success. They don't grow fast. They don't have much money. Most of the important people don't attend small churches. They usually don't have exciting and innovative programs of ministry to the community. They are not on the cutting edge of theology. By every measurable standard, small churches are unsuccessful. Therefore, they are a bit of an embarrassment to the denomination.

Secondly, small churches are expensive. It is very expensive for church judicatories annually to supplement the salaries of each small church pastor by three to ten thousand dollars to meet minimum standards. And with rising inflation, this trend promises to get much worse. Small churches will continue to be even more expensive in the future. They may eventually become the single, largest economic drain on the major denominations of America. The small church is expensive.

Finally, the greatest problem of the small church is the people who belong to them. Members of small churches

1

are usually hostile and unresponsive to the denomination. They are suspicious and will seldom follow expectations and guidelines like they should. They are rarely willing to make sensible compromises, and they resist any and all changes. Persons in small churches are usually hostile and unresponsive to the denomination.

Therefore, the small church is a problem, a very serious problem, for most denominations. And no strategy seems to help. There are just too many small churches to close them all. Mergers never seem to work. And whatever strategy is designed, from benign neglect to overconcern, the situation never really seems to change. These small churches remain about the same size, doing about the same things that they have always done. And that makes the small church a very big problem.

The Unique Character of the Small Church

There is one basic reason why the small church is viewed as a problem by pastors, denominational executives, and judicatories. The small church is not understood. For the small church is different. It is a totally unique kind of organism. And unless this is clearly understood by pastors, executives, and judicatories alike, the small church will certainly remain a problem.

The small church as an institution is really a holdover from a past era of American society. Whether in an urban area, a small town or open country area, the small church that we hear so much about today is an institution which embodies the values of America's rural, frontier past. It is an institution which has insulated itself from some of the drastic changes of modern industrialized society, in order to preserve some of the traditional, relational values of the past. And because some of these values are so important to so many people, the small

2

church will probably continue to be an important institution within many parts of our society, for years to come.

There are several unique characteristics of the small church which need to be understood from the outset. Some of these have been previously pointed out by Professor Carl Dudley of McCormick Seminary in his book *Making the Small Church Effective*. Most helpful has been his discussion of the small church as a "Caring Cell."[1]

It is important to recognize that small churches are often intentionally small. The small church must remain small, or change its character. I believe the optimum size for a small church to be somewhere around 150 members. That is about the maximum size for a group in which all the members can know one another.

When I say that the small church is intentionally small, I don't mean that its smallness is objectively planned. But certainly subconsciously most members in small congregations do not want their church to get too large. They want to know everyone in the group. That's the most important ingredient of a small church.

I've done some statistical studies of some of the small churches in our Presbytery that periodically have experienced periods of growth. They will grow to between 100 and 150 members, and then growth ceases. Either they become static, or the church splits. That may not be by conscious design, but in most instances I believe it to be unavoidable. Persons who participate in small churches are there because they are small. That is the main attraction. And if they go beyond that inherent optimum size limit, the basic nature changes.

What this means, of course, is that the small church is based primarily upon human relationships. And in most instances that means kinship relationships. The prototype of the small church today is to be found in rural areas. The small rural church emerged from small com-

3

munities that were based upon kinship ties. That being the case, everyone in such small churches knows everyone else. They know each other not just by name, either. They know the entire family history of everyone else. The small churches of today are often based upon this kind of kinship relationship.

This means that structurally the small church is different. Most small churches are based upon a horizontal social structure as opposed to the vertical social structure of modern urban society. Horizontal social relationships are interactions between relative equals, while vertical social relationships are social interactions in which one group or individual possess higher status and more power than the others, and is therefore in the position to control the others.

In most small churches it is important that everyone appears to be equal. That does not mean that there aren't those who exercise control and power in small churches. But it does mean that those who have the power and control usually don't like to flaunt it. They want to appear to be like everyone else.

It also means that the power and control that they possess has been invested through history and traditional family ties. Everyone recognizes who holds the power, but few talk much about it. In normal day to day interactions, those who have power want to be like everyone else. But when important decisions are made, they are the ones who are consulted first.

Therefore, in small churches, important decisions are made by concensus, not by democratic vote. Regardless of who sits on the church boards as elected officials, there are certain persons in the congregation who must be consulted before the decision is made. They are the ones who have been invested with authority by tradition and family ties.

The small church is not only structurally different; it

also embodies a host of values that emerge from past rural society.

History and tradition are exceptionally important. It is not necessarily the written history of data and dates that is important. Rather, it is the remembered history of people and artifacts that embody memories and experiences. Certain ways of doing things become sacred ritual in small churches, because they embody tradition and memory. Certain favorite hymns may seem theologically unsound, but they carry important memories and feelings, and they are therefore highly valued by the people.

The whole concept of sacred space and time is real in many small churches. This is best understood as one looks at primitive societies. In primitive societies the sacred is the center of life. Sacred time and space become important means of enabling people to experience the sacred through symbolic representations. For instance, primitive peoples organize all life around space. Sacred space consists of those places, those physical, geographic points, where a person can enter the realm of the sacred and where the sacred will pass into the world of man.

To lesser degrees this concept of sacred space is still part of the world view of many small church people, especially those in rural areas. In the minds of church members, the church building serves the symbolic function of being sacred space. "For a believer the church shares in a different space from the street in which it stands. The door that opens on the interior of the church actually signifies a solution of continuity. The threshold that separates the two spaces, also indicates the distance between two modes of being, the profane and the religious."[2]

The church building in rural communities is often the geographic center of the town, or is located on a hill in a place of high visibility. Symbolically, religion becomes the center of life at all times.

Understanding the concept of time is no less important. Among the people of small rural congregations there are really three concepts of time. They are measured time, appropriate time and sacred time.

Measured time is the schedule of time, the minutes on the clock, the dates on the calendar. Modern industrialized society runs by measured time. Meetings are begun on schedule at a certain, specified time. Commitments in the date book must be kept.

Rural people live more according to appropriate time. Meetings do not necessarily start at the appointed moment, unless all the people who are coming are present. It's inappropriate to start a meeting at 7:30 if you know that George will be there within the next ten minutes. George is more important than the specific time of the meeting. Small church people often have a firm concept of the appropriateness of time.

In addition there are also sacred times, times of special religious significance. In a very real sense the time of the Sunday morning worship service can be a sacred time. It is an interval that breaks from the mundane, in which the individual is more apt to encounter God. Why? Because it has always been so.

Certain seasonal celebrations may have the force of sacred time also. And they may not be the traditional church celebrations of Christmas and Easter. The sacred times for a small rural congregation may include Mother's Day, Memorial Day and Thanksgiving Day. For these are the times which traditionally have been set aside as periods of special celebration. Small church people often experientially recognize sacred time and space.

In the final analysis the small church generally has a different primary reason for being than does a large church. People in small churches do not envision the primary role of the church as doing program. The church exists to undergird community. The church is to *be,* not just to do. The small church is a relational organism, rather than an organization. When viewed and understood as such, the small church takes on a wholly different light.

Having said all of that, it is important to recognize that many small churches do have a common problem. Not all, for there are some that are very vital. But many do have the problem of being so preoccupied with survival, institutional survival, that they are immobilized. And they are preoccupied with survival for a very good reason. Their survival has been threatened. The threat of institutional survival, of keeping a pastor, of paying the bills, of having enough people to ensure the future, is an ever present threat for many small churches.

Related to that is the feeling of defeatism. Most small church people recognize that their church is not successful by denominational standards. They are different from those larger churches in the cities. They aren't doing a whole lot of programs. When those annual evaluation forms are filled out, indeed they can feel very out of step, and weak, and hopeless. And that can be a very real problem that could eventually lead to the death of many small congregations. Indeed many have already experienced dissolution and death during the past half century.

This need not be the case. I believe that many small churches can experience revitalization, and rediscover new identity and a sense of mission. And it is the task of the denominational judicatories and the pastors of such congregations to enable this process of revitalization to occur.

However, before this process of revitalization can begin to occur, there needs to be a much clearer understanding of how the small church of today has evolved to its present state of being. The purpose of this book is to examine the roots of the small church in America to gain a better understanding of how it evolved into this unique institution in modern American society. Based upon this analysis it will then be my intention to propose a planned process of revitalization for small churches aimed ultimately at recovering that truly unique ministry of undergirding community life.

Chapter One Notes

1. Carl S. Dudley, *Making the Small Church Effective* (Nashville: Abingdon, 1978), p. 32.

2. Micea Eliade, *The Sacred and the Profane* (New York: Harper and Row, 1961), p. 25.

Part I

Historical Foundations
of the
Small Church Today

CHAPTER TWO

The Church and the Community

There are historical reasons why small churches often seem to be weak and to lack identity. There seems little doubt that the small church of today emerged as a result of the transition of our society from rural agrarian life to urban industrialized life.

The small church originated as the central institution of rural life in American society. In urban areas, the small church originated as an ethnic or neighborhood church. In both instances the small church's primary reason for being was to undergird community. The transition to modern, heterogeneous industrialized society, undercut that original unique purpose of the small church.

In this section of the book we will be looking at some of the historical roots of the small rural church to gain a clearer perspective of what this transition has meant. We will specifically be dealing with that transition as it occurred in rural Appalachia, for rural Appalachia serves as the prototype and clearest example of what this transition has meant for the small church elsewhere.

In making this overview it is not the intent to make value judgments regarding whether preindustrialized or postindustrialized society was better. The purpose is rather to understand the extent of trauma and social upheaval that occurred, and to assess its affects upon the small church.

Before dealing with that history of transition, however, it is first necessary to gain a common understanding of what is meant when I speak of the church as the center of community, and specifically what is meant by community.

There seems to be little unanimity of opinion of what community is, or what its functions are. For the purpose of this book, I will be approaching community from the standpoint of a small group of people, living in relationship with one another, who act cooperatively to meet individual and group needs.

Perhaps a formal definition will help to clarify the concept.

"A community is an association of individuals and families that out of inclination, habit, custom, and mutual interest, act in concert as a unit in meeting their common needs . . . to whatever extent common group needs are met by unified action in a spirit of common acquaintance and responsibility, to that extent community exists."[1]

This somewhat classical definition of community that emphasizes geographic space, small size, common way of life, and cooperative and collective action to meet group needs, of necessity places community in a rural sphere. Or if urban life is the setting for community, it is a subgroup within the city.

For the purpose of this book, there are two essential aspects of community which must be understood. One is the aspect of human relationships. The second is the function of community.

Both relationship and function are essential to community. It is also a fact that in modern industrialized society, function has become preeminent. This is one of the most distinguishing characteristics that separates modern life from societies of the past.

The contrast between relationally based community

12

life, and industrialized society which is oriented toward function and production is explained by the concepts of "Gemeinschaft and Gesellschaft" in the writing of Tonnes, and the concepts of "Communal and Associative" communities in the writings of Max Weber. These conceptual terms emerged in nineteenth century Europe to describe the transition from rural to industrialized society.

In Gemeinschaft, or the relationally based community of traditional rural society, community rests upon kinship, turf and friendship. In Weber's writings for instance, "a relationship is communal when it is based on a subjective feeling of the parties that they belong to each other, that they are implicated in each other's total existence."[2] Society functions to meet human need, but the function is secondary to and totally dependent upon the health of the communal relationships.

Modern industrialized society, on the other hand, has produced Gesellschaft or the associative community. Community has been rationally constructed for the purpose of production. Society is no longer primarily based upon human relationships. It exists to function. And all institutions within society have been affected by that change.

For Tonnes, "The theory of Gesellschaft deals with the artificial construction of an aggregate of human beings which superficially resembles the Gemeinschaft (society based upon kinship) insofar as the individuals live and dwell peacefully. However, in Gemeinschaft they remain essentially united in spite of all separating factors, whereas in Gesellschaft they are essentially separated in spite of all uniting factors."[3]

In these early sociological writings then, there emerges a basic understanding of community and society that contrasts rural, kinship, and land-based community, with urban, industrialized, production-based society. For the purpose of this study I will be using the term community to apply to the rural-based concept of community in which relationships between people are primary.

It is in the writings of Martin Buber that the essential connecting link of community relationships is defined. In his book *Paths in Utopia*, Buber discusses his concept of community, and concludes that the foundation of community life and community relationships is the spiritual tie of common faith that binds people together.

> The real essence of community is to be found in the fact—manifest or otherwise—that it has a center. The real beginning of a community is when its members have a common relation to the center overriding all other relations: the circle is described by the radii, not by the points along its circumference. And the originality of the center cannot be discerned unless it is discerned as being transpicuous to the light of something divine.[4]

This is an essential understanding. One principal contention discussed throughout this study is that faith, i.e., religion, forms the foundation of community. It is through the common faith commitment of a group of people that personal relationships are affirmed and undergirded, and community life comes into existence.

A secondary understanding of this study is that community exists to meet human need. This includes the whole realm of human need including economic, psychological, and spiritual needs. To whatever degree human needs are met through cooperation and reciprocity, based upon a common faith commitment, to that degree community exists.

All communities then, exist in a state of dynamic tension between being and doing. The foundation of community is people being in relationship with one another, with their lives centering on a common faith commitment. At the same time, flowing out of this relationship is a life of working and doing together, in order to meet common needs.

How does religion per se serve as the center of community? Traditionally, throughout the history of humanity, there have been several distinct functions of religion that have provided an undergirding for community life.

First is the common belief system. The belief system of a community explains its origins and purpose, and forms the common commitment of the people. The belief system gives moral sanction to the social structure of the community. It likewise provides a means of personal identification. The individual discovers self in relationship to community and the history and beliefs of the groups. Therefore, religious belief forms the basis of community life and the life of the individual.

Community ceremony and ritual is always grounded in the religion, that common faith commitment. Worship is the principal means of reenergizing community life. True community celebrations always center on the common faith commitment of the people, and serve to solidify the group and reenergize it. Members of the community receive power, energy and meaning in the midst of the community celebrations.

Religion gives validation to the cyclical rhythms of life through its ritual ceremonies. The principal crisis points of human life, birth, puberty, marriage, and death are externalized and given validation through community ritual ceremony. This serves to further enable each member of the community to maintain identity in the context of community.

Next, in traditional societies of the past, religion has always been a means of leveling, and leveling is one of the primary means of social stability. Confronted by God, all community members are equal.

Related to that, in most traditional societies of the

past, religion has had the function of economically redistributing the wealth. Religion normally gives the basis for economic cooperation to ensure that all community members receive the necessities of life.

These are some of the basic functions that religion has traditionally played in community life. Community cannot exist without some common belief system, some common faith commitment. Religion is the glue that holds community together.

The basic assumption of this study is then, that the small church emerged in rural American society as the center of community life. It provided the primary connecting link, and embodied the common faith commitment, that held people together in community. And it was the subsequent loss of this basic, natural function that has left many small churches today, adrift and searching for identity as congregations.

Chapter Two Notes

1. Arthur E. Morgan, *The Small Community* (New York: Harper and Brothers, 1942), p. 20.

2. Robert A. Nisbet, *The Sociological Tradition* (New York: Basic Books, Inc., 1966), p. 80.

3. Ibid., p. 75.

4. Martin Buber, *Paths in Utopia* (Boston: Beacon Press, 1970), p. 135.

CHAPTER THREE

The Frontier Church

It is now necessary for us to focus our attention on what we shall term the frontier church. (The specific focus of the study will be the emergence of the frontier church in Appalachia.) For it is with the frontier church that we gain a fairly clear picture how at one point in the history of that region, religion became the center of community life. By the frontier church we shall mean the rural and small town churches that emerged in Appalachia before the Civil War.

At the outset when white settlers and fur trappers first came into the wilderness, there was an extended period in which there were no organized churches.

> The point is that the church—Calvinist, Anglican, or radical sect—was wholly unprepared to follow the emigrant and his sons westward with the disorderly and rampaging frontier. The vicars, parsons, the priests and preachers would have recoiled from frontier conditions as fire withdraws from water, and the frontier was a hundred years old before any serious effort was made to give spiritual instruction to its sons and daughters.[1]

In the intervening period the frontiersman, who was often illiterate, was without any formal religious instruction. What religion there was, passed on from generation to generation by oral tradition.

> Thus the frontiersman was cast adrift in a wilderness with a garble of Christian tradition and half-remembered beliefs.

17

> Unable to find fulfillment for inevitable spiritual needs at the altar and without priest, parson, or preacher to console him, he turned in many instances to his old enemy and teacher—the red man.[2]

It was in this manner that Indian traditions, and the dualistic view of a Sacred and Profane universe, entered the belief system of the frontier white settler. And it was at this point a great deal of Indian lore concerning the raising of crops, and cures for illnesses also entered the traditions of the mountaineers.

Theology on the Appalachian Frontier

Following the Revolutionary War a new migration of settlers moved into the mountain wilderness of Appalachia and scattered towns and villages began to grow up. It was with this migration that organized religion in the form of the circuit rider began to play an important role for the first time. Many of these early settlers were of Scotch-Irish Presbyterian tradition. When formalized religion did begin to have its influence on the frontier, it was through Baptist, Presbyterian and Methodist circuit riders who formed congregations in the more densely settled areas, and returned periodically to hold services. Both the Methodist and Presbyterian preachers were strongly influenced by Calvinistic theology. It was therefore inevitable that most of these frontier churches would be heavily influenced by Calvinism and the theology of John Wesley.

There were several key elements of Calvinistic theology that were accommodated to the frontier religion which had a lasting affect on the nature of religion in the mountains. The first was the Calvinistic emphasis upon individualism, which combined with Wesley's emphasis upon "holiness," laid particularly strong emphasis upon the mystical conversion experience. It was with this emphasis upon the conversion experience that revivalism became such an important part of frontier religion.

The frontier settlers were strongly individualistic, or they never would have migrated to the wilderness. Calvinism merely supported their felt beliefs. Connected to the individualism was the strong belief that each person could interpret religion for himself, and a genuine resentment of anyone who tried to impose religious beliefs on anyone else.

The second important component of frontier theology that emerged from Calvinism was the emphasis upon sin. The frontier revivals always focused a great deal of attention on the sinfulness of the individual in very vivid terms. Specific sins of personal immorality were emphasized, along with the admonition to help one's neighbor.

The Calvinistic emphasis upon predestination in many instances became overshadowed by the Baptist emphasis upon free will, and Wesley's view of sanctification. In each case, preaching on the frontier emphasized the need for confession of sins and a change of life, or the individual would be confronted with God's eternal damnation.

The third great emphasis from Calvinistic theology which only gradually had its effect upon frontier religion was community. With the sparsity of towns and villages, frontier society was originally very family oriented with little emphasis upon town. It was with the founding of towns, that formal churches and a broader sense of community began to emerge. And when villages and communities did grow up around churches, they very often did reflect the Calvinistic emphasis of religion as the central focus of community life.

Finally, there was an element in the theology of frontier settlers that was quite foreign to Calvinism, but which accommodated itself more easily to Methodism which was less systematic and rationalistic. This was the carry-over from the earliest days of frontier life, of primitive Indian dualism. It was natural, no doubt, that this emphasis would emerge in a wilderness, rural area in which life revolved around hunting and farming. At any rate, incorporated into the individualistic religion of the frontier was a somewhat mystical view of nature, and a dualistic emphasis upon a Sacred/Profane cosmos.

General Characteristics of the Frontier Church

It is most difficult to gain a clear picture of what the rural frontier church in Appalachia was like. However, it is possible through studying the histories of individual congregations and other sources to begin to pull together a few characteristics which these churches seem to have had in common.

We have previously mentioned that there was an emerging belief system among frontier Christians. Generally Christianity on the frontier emphasized an individualized religion with a focus upon the conversion experience and personal sin, coupled with a somewhat mystical dualism.

As churches began to spring up in villages and towns, a second characteristic began to emerge, that of denominational cooperation. Speaking of this general characteristic that began to pervade American Protestantism at this time, it is recognized that:

> A distinctive "American" type of Christianity began to emerge. It was built around a solid core of Puritanism, especially as represented by Congregationalists and Presbyterians, but including also Baptists and Low Church Episcopalians, plus additions from the Reformed and Methodists, and even from the less closely related Lutherans. This was the "benevolent empire" in which individuals, but not church bodies, co-operated in voluntary societies for missionary, educational, and reforming activities. Revivalism was its characteristic tool. The doctrine of the church which was implied in this benevolent empire bor-

rowed heavily from Congregationalism. Congregationalism's doctrine of the invisible church, in which all true Christians are already one, greatly encouraged nondenominational cooperation, and Congregationalism's teaching that the term visible church was not applicable to denominational bodies, but only to local congregations or to universal Christendom, discouraged emphasis on denominations as such.[3]

We have previously mentioned that Baptist, Methodists, and Presbyterians were the first denominations to evangelize the frontier and start congregations. No denomination had the financial resources to pay for pastoral leadership in all of the churches that began to emerge on the frontier. The circuit riders were sent into these towns and rural areas to start churches and serve them on a rotating basis. Preaching services might be held once a month at the most.

As it happened, Methodist, Presbyterian, and Baptist circuit riders often established congregations in the same locality. To save on expenses, usually only one church building was erected and then was used by all the congregations.

In addition, since the individual circuit riders came to the church only once a month at the most, everyone from all congregations attended preaching services whenever they were held. In this way services continued on a fairly regular basis.

What developed was sort of a defacto ecumenism whereby a community was provided with preaching services on a rotating basis by preachers of different denominations. This did not always abet a uniform system of doctrine, but it did enhance the concept of a church being based not upon denomination, but upon a community of people.

The third major characteristic of the frontier church was that of revivalism. Revivals were always important aspects of religion on the frontier. They were the principal means through which new converts were brought into the church, and in general they served an energizing function for the entire community.

Revivalism on the frontier was highly emotional and at times almost paralleled the tribal celebrations of primitive societies. They were often held in the spring and fall and afforded the opportunity for community seasonal celebrations that broke the regular routine of life. The camp meeting soon became the prototype, with revivals lasting for a week or two weeks at a time. Usually, families from all over the vicinity would travel to the camp meeting revival and stay the entire week.

Describing the occurrences at a camp meeting revival in eastern Kentucky in 1801, a colonel Robert Patterson of Lexington, Kentucky, related the following tale:

> On the 1st of May, at a society on the waters of Fleming creek, on the east side of Licking, a boy, under the age of twelve years, became affected in an extraordinary manner, publicly confessing and acknowledging his sins, praying for pardon, through Christ, and recommending Jesus Christ to sinners, as being ready to save the vilest of the vile—Adult persons became affected in the like manner. The flame began to spread, the Sabbath following, at Mr. Camble's Meeting House—a number became affected. The third Sabbath of May, on Cabin creek, six miles above Limestone, the Sacrament of the Lord's Supper was administered by Mr. Camble and Mr. M'Namaar, at which time about sixty persons were struck down. Next Sabbath, on Fleming creek, under Mr. M'Namaar, and Mr. Camble, on a like occasion, about 100 persons were struck down and deeply convinced. The first Sabbath of June, Mr. Stone administered the Lord's Supper, in Concord congregation on the head-waters of Kingston, in the bounds of which exercises of the same kind had made their appearance in society, and at sermon. On Friday night preceding the Sacrament at Concord, I was present at a society, held at Kainridge, a united congregation of Mr. Stone, and saw the extraordinary work. Of fifty persons present, nine were struck down. I proceeded next morning to Concord, ten miles distance, where a sermon was preached, at which several became affected and struck down. The exercises continued all

night. This was the first occasion, that shewed the necessity of performing out doors. The number being so great, the Lord's Supper was administered at a tent. A great solemity [sic] appeared all day. A number were struck down; on the whole occasion about 150. The exercises continued from Saturday till Wednesday, day and night, without intermission. The appearance itself was awful and solemn. It was performed in a thick grove of beachen timber; candles were furnished by the congregation. The night still and calm. Add to that, exhortations, praying, singing, the cries of the distressed, on account of sin; the rejoicing of those, that were delivered from their sin's bondage, and brought to enjoy the liberty that is in Christ Jesus; all going on at the same time. About 4000 persons attended, 250 communicated; twelve waggons had brought some of the people with their provisions, and from distant places. This was the first occasion that shewed the necessity of encamping on the ground; the neighborhood not being able to furnish strangers with accommodation; nor had they a wish to separate.[4]

The camp meeting was, of course, not the only type of revivalism on the frontier. On the local community level, revivals were held at regular intervals, and they were always highlights of the life of the community. The emphasis was upon individual conversion it is true, but there was also always a strong social emphasis upon helping one's neighbor that accompanied it. It was partly through revivalism that a true sense of community spirit and morality was born and reinforced.

A fourth characteristic of the frontier church in the mountains was that it was usually the center of community life. Churches were normally constructed in the center of town, or a place of high visibility, so that even geographically they could serve as a center of focus. The social life of the community often revolved around church basket dinners and the like. There were points when the church became the locus for discussing community issues.

Leadership and decision making within the local congregation was usually on a congregational basis, even in

Presbyterian and Methodist churches. Decisions were made when the congregation gathered for services, and the real influence and authority rested with the male members of the congregation, although women always had a strong voice in church activities, too.

Another characteristic is the fact that there was usually no regular, ordained clergy available. The circuit riders came through the village only periodically. Therefore, very early in the life of the frontier church, congregations began to depend upon lay preachers to lead worship. And in many respects the lay preacher offered the only real pastoral care that the congregation experienced.

In the early 1800s the Sunday school began to emerge as another important influence in mountain churches. The Sunday school movement began in England in the late eighteenth century as an alternative for public education for poor children who had to work during the week. However, the concept of Sunday school soon became adapted as the principal means of religious education for children in the church.

By the 1820s and 1830s Sunday schools were being formed in churches on the frontier and in many instances a great portion of the church life of the community began to revolve around the Sunday school. It became the means by which the Bible was taught to the children, and it served as the focus for the congregation gathering on a regular basis, rather than waiting for when the circuit rider would make his rounds.

To the present day, the Sunday school has remained as one of the most important facets of small rural churches in the region.

Rural communities in the area had a horizontal social structure, and this was certainly reinforced through the church. Once conversion occurred and an individual was saved, that person was accepted into the community on

24

an equal basis with all others. Therefore, the frontier church served as a leveling influence within the local community.

The Frontier Preacher

We have previously mentioned that churches on the frontier were generally served by circuit riding preachers who held services at churches on a rotating basis. The Methodists under Bishop Asbury developed the most effective system of circuit riding. The frontier was divided into geographic areas with a circuit rider assigned to each area. He was financially supported by the Methodist denomination and was able to give all of his time to this endeavor. Since the Methodists did not have restrictions of higher education as did the Presbyterians, the Methodist preacher could often relate to the frontier family much more effectively.

The Presbyterian ministers usually settled in a community and served a smaller circuit of churches. They normally had to augment their income in some fashion, oftentimes by establishing and teaching at a frontier school.

> Presbyterian ministers were invariably men of learning—many came from Princeton, the great intellectual stronghold of the church, hundreds of whose graduates entered the ministry in the century before the Civil War. On the frontier they sought out communities of their own kind (the Scotch-Irish) and this, together with the strictness of their religious doctrines, limited their influence on the mass of men.[5]

The question of educated clergy was a problem that haunted the Presbyterian denomination for years. It was this question of education, in fact, that helped precipitate several splits within the Presbyterian church on the frontier.

Within Presbyterianism, revivalism aroused considerable determined opposition. The frontier Presbyterian revivalists tended to be less concerned with maintaining standards of an educated ministry and less committed to the full cycle of Calvinist doctrine than was the denomination as a whole, and especially that part of it in which the Scotch-Irish tradition was strong. In Kentucky, efforts on the part of Presbyterian leaders to bring the revivalists into conformity led to several separations. Barton W. Stone (1772-1844) led the "New Light" schism in 1803. At first he and his associates formed an independent Presbytery; but they soon dissolved this, and abandoning all "sectarian" names, they took only the name "Christian". In 1810, revivalists of the Cumberland (Kentucky) Presbytery organized themselves into an independent body, which six years later adopted the name Cumberland Presbyterian Church.[6]

It is impossible to depict a prototype of the frontier preacher, but generally they did have a few things in common. By and large, most were ordinary folk, raised on the frontier, who, even if they possessed some higher education, could speak the language of the common people.

Even if Presbyterian, they often did not emphasize the Calvinistic doctrines of total depravity, election, and predestination, and, like Barton Stone, preached that "God loved the whole world and had sent His Son to save all men if they would but believe, and that sinners were capable of fulfilling that condition."[7] However, we can at the same time be assured that the concept of a personal call to preach was strongly felt.

The frontier preacher was seldom able to become pastor of a single congregation. His ministry with churches included occasional preaching services, administration of the sacraments, weddings, funerals, and extensive visitation with families when in the area. With the exception of the Methodist circuit rider, he often farmed or taught school to supplement his income. The principal criteria were that he feel a sense of call, be an adequate preacher, and care about people. The frontier preachers and circuit riders often spent their entire ministry in this rural setting.

The Structure of Rural Society and the Function of Religion on the Appalachian Frontier

Up to this point we have focused attention on religion in general on the Appalachian frontier. As a concluding thought something needs to be said about the general structure of society in Appalachia at this time, and the function played by religion.

In the earliest days of the Appalachian frontier, life was dominated by hunters and trappers. Later the small family homesteads became important, and small towns and villages began to grow up as trading centers. Life still centered very much on the family unit.

It has been assumed by some historians and sociologists that community life was fairly much absent from frontier society in much of Appalachia and western Virginia prior to the dawn of industrialization. It is true that in what is now southern Appalachia there were few towns. Many frontier families lived in isolation from one another. However, it does not necessarily follow that community did not exist.

Kinship is the primary basis of community, not a narrow geographic locale with a concentration of families. The frontier of southwestern Virginia was originally settled by families of Scotch-Irish background. Emerging from this Scotch-Irish tradition, it can be stated with certainty that kinship and clan became the basis of community, much as in more primitive tribal societies. Individual family units occupied homesteads in mountain hollows and valley areas. Extended family groups settled in the same general geographic area. Community structure and solidarity was based upon kinship relations.

There was certainly cooperative action aimed at meeting mutual needs through the extended family. In addition, such gatherings as barn raisings indicate that cooperative action frequently extended beyond the bounds of kinship.

Finally, there is little doubt that community kinship relations were undergirded by religion. Community worship was more of a seasonal event than a regularly weekly or monthly occurrence. The center of religious practice was the individual family unit. The family Bible, for instance, occupied a place of particular prominence in most frontier homes. The seasonal camp meeting revivals offer an interesting parallel to the tradition of the gathering of the clans of Scotland. Therefore, even on the isolated frontier of Southwestern Virginia prior to the emergence of towns, community was real, based upon kinship relations, and undergirded by religion.

Very gradually, between 1800 and 1860 village and town life began to assume a more important place in the mountains, and by the time of the Civil War the small town had become the center of community in many parts of Appalachia.

The preponderance of population still lived on small farms and homesteads, but people began to focus more importance on the local town as a trading center and a locus for social activity. The general store, school, and local church were all important centers of community life.

The small Appalachian village of this antebellum era, like most rural towns of the past, generally had a horizontal social structure. The individual received a sense of personal identity and worth, not from status related to occupation, but from kinship.

In many respects the small, rural town in Appalachia

prior to the Civil War was closely akin to our previous definition of community used in chapter two. And as we have already seen, religion was of singular importance in solidifying community life and undergirding the entire social structure.

The church of rural Appalachia at this time did offer a fairly unified belief system. As we have previously seen the principal emphases were upon personal sin, the individual conversion experience, personal morality, and concern for neighbor. This provided a firm undergirding for local community life.

Worship, with its strong emphasis upon revivalism, served a reenergizing function for both the individual and the community. And more often than not the revivals were seasonal celebrations coming in the spring and fall.

Religion again served a leveling function, by emphasizing the universality of sin and the need for personal conversion by everyone. In addition, the church was often the institution through which the redistribution of wealth occurred. Frontier revivalism gave impetus to this, for coupled with the message of personal salvation was always the admonition to help one's neighbor in need.

The frontier church was in many respects responsible for education on the community level. As has previously been pointed out, the local preacher was sometimes also the local teacher. And the Presbyterian church was usually instrumental in the establishment of local schools when public education was not available.

In conclusion, it can be stated with assurance that the rural frontier church played a major role in the life of the small rural communities in Appalachia prior to the Civil War.

Chapter Three Notes

1. Harry M. Caudill, *Night Comes to the Cumberlands* (Boston: Little, Brown and Company, 1961), p. 25.

2. Ibid., p. 26.

3. H. Shelton Smith, Robert T. Handy, and Lefferts A. Leetscher, *American Christianity—An Historical Interpretation with Representative Documents* (New York: Charles Scribner's Sons, 1960), vol. 2, pp. 66-67.

4. Ibid., vol. 1, p. 567.

5. Robert Wallace, "The Rugged Basis of American Protestantism," *Life Magazine*, Time-Life Publications, Chicago, December 26, 1955, p. 73.

6. Op. cit., Smith, vol. 1, p. 563.

7. Kenneth Scott Latourette, *A History of Christianity* (New York: Harper and Brothers, 1953), p. 1041.

CHAPTER FOUR

The Industrialization of Appalachia

The Industrialization of the Region

The Civil War marked the dividing line for a basic change in the nature of community and religion in Appalachia. Until this point in history, life in the mountains had been community based and had gradually begun to center on the small, rural town. In one sense this trend continued after the Civil War. But the major change that occurred was that the nature and structure of the rural Appalachian town was totally transformed. In the process, the function of religion was drastically altered.

The force that precipitated this dramatic change was the intrusion of industrialization into the mountains.

One result of the War Between the States was a shift in the balance of power from the Southern agrarian based economy, to the Northern industrialized economy. As a result the development of industrialization went almost unchecked for forty years. Before rapid industrialization could occur there had to be a ready source of cheap natural resources. The lumber and coal deposits of the Appalachian Mountains loomed as a ripe plum ready to be plucked.

As appealing as these resources were, the region was almost inaccessible until the post-Civil War era. Some means of transporting raw materials to the industrial centers had to be developed. The construction of the Shay engine in the 1850s ensured that the railroads could become that means of transporting raw materials.

The first obstacle that had to be overcome was control of the land. Therefore in the years immediately following the Civil War, land agents were sent into Appalachia by lumber and railroad companies to gain control of the land.

> The Companies began to operate through County-seat merchants and court house officials whom they took into their confidence and employed to buy timber tracts on a commission basis. These men spoke the language of the mountaineers and were more likely to be believed when they assured him that his trees were of little value and that he and his descendants might never again have an opportunity to trade them for cash.[1]

The same tactic was used a few years later to lay claim to the coal lands. Land often was sold at as little as five to ten cents an acre and sometimes less. Other land agents purchased only the mineral, timber, and access rights to the land, and this often worked even more to their advantage.

> The goal was to buy minerals on a grand scale as cheaply as possible and on terms so favorable to the purchasers as to grant them every desirable exploitive privilege, while simultaneously leaving the mountaineer with the illusion of ownership and the continuing responsibility for practicaly [sic] all the taxes which thereafter might be levied against the land.[2]

In north central West Virginia where I now reside, Henry G. Davis and Stephen B. Elkins were the principal industrialists who developed the coal, lumber, and railroad industries. Stephen Elkins was a land lawyer of considerable reputation who later became a U.S. Senator, and Henry G. Davis was a railroad builder, and coal and lumber entrepreneur, who had previously served in the Senate. In developing their enterprises in West Virginia, Davis took charge of railroad and company town construction. Elkins set up a law office in New York to clear land titles, and handle other legal transactions. "Of course his primary purpose in going to the populace city was to set up an office from which he would dispose of tracts of land and shares in his mining stock."[3] Through their cooperative endeavors, they gradually gained control of the political and economic sphere of north central West Virginia.

The point is that between 1865 and 1890, two major changes occurred throughout much of Appalachia. First, ownership of land and mineral rights changed hands from local homesteaders to industrialists with large corporate holdings. Secondly, the railroad was built into the mountains to provide a means of transporting raw materials to the industrial centers of the Northeastern United States.

The next steps that served to transform the nature and structure of life in Appalachia were the construction of company towns and the importation of labor.

By 1890 a coal mine could be started with a relatively small amount of capital. The coal mine operator could begin with a capital investment of twenty to thirty thousand dollars which he could usually borrow from the county seat bank. The principal investment was in building homes for the workers. Since many of the mines were located in isolated areas, and it was necessary for the miners to live fairly close to the mine, houses had to be built for the workers to live in. The typical house was a three- or four-room cabin that cost approximately fifty dollars to build. So if a mine operator hired one hundred workers, his initial capital outlay for housing would be about five thousand dollars.[4]

The ready source of labor in West Virginia and throughout Appalachia at this point in history was relatively scarce. There were some homesteaders who were willing to move into company towns and work in the mines or lumber mills, but many preferred to stay on their farms.

Therefore, the companies began to look elsewhere for a new labor force. They looked first to the new influx of immigrants crowding the Eastern cities as a quick source of cheap labor. Some companies cooperated in financing immigrant ships to bring these workers from the Old World to America. Elaborate brochures, picturing the economic advantages of working in America were prepared. These advertisements were sent to the Eastern cities and to Europe telling of the idyllic life and unparalleled opportunities for advancement offered by working in the mines. Complete passage to West Virginia was paid by the company, and the immigrants were promised a house to live in, and a job upon their arrival.

Another ready source of labor were the blacks of the South. Many black laborers had been hired by the railroads for building new railways into the mountain wilderness. Having completed their construction tasks they were available to be hired to work in the mines. In addition, representatives from the coal companies were sent into the South to recruit workers, and bring them to the company towns by rail. Howard Lee relates the following concerning the importation of workers:

> The train was in the complete control of the agents, and the coach doors were kept locked until it arrived at its destination. This was for the protection of the passengers, many of whom were having their first train ride. An agent once told me that he believed that it was the prospect of the train ride, rather than the promise of steady work at high wages, that induced many of his passengers to leave their southern homes.[5]

As this new labor source began to invade Appalachia, more of the original settlers began to be attracted away from the farm to try to earn their fortune in the coal and lumber towns. Therefore, in the space of twenty to thirty years Appalachia, and West Virginia and Kentucky in particular, began to be transformed from a rural based frontier society of homesteads and small towns, to a rural industrialized area of burgeoning coal camps and mill towns. The entire structure of society quickly began to change.

The Rationale for the Company Town

There is little doubt that most coal operators felt justified in building coal camps. The building of such industrial towns was absolutely essential if coal mining was to prove practicable in Appalachia.

The typical coal camp house was a four- or five-room Jenny Lind Cabin. As previously stated, the company could build these houses for between $50.00 and $75.00 each, and charge a modest rent to the worker and his family for living in the house. In 1900 rents for these cabins varied from $1.50 to $2.50 per room per month. Therefore, the maximum rent paid for a five-room house was about $12.50 per month.

In addition, the company was responsible for the upkeep of the house, and for a fee provided the family with utilities (water and electricity when it became available). This provided relatively inexpensive housing for the workers, and at the same time, within six to eight months the company would receive its initial housing investment back, through rents.

"To the mountaineers in whose midst such homes sprang up, they (the coal company house) were palatial, and rumors spread with wildfire speed throughout the Plateau that 'fine homes were being built by the hundreds'."[6] Therefore, the company usually had little difficulty enticing native workers to move into the camp and work in the mines.

Since these early coal towns were quite isolated, there was an obvious need for a general store to provide for the material needs of the workers. Therefore, early in the life of these coal towns, company stores began to be built. The miners generally received fairly low pay, and the living expenses sometimes exceeded incomes. Therefore, a system of credit needed to be established. As a result, the practice of issuing scrip as a means of extending credit to the workers was instituted.

> Much misunderstanding has been circulated—often deliberately—about the operation of the company store. The true situation was quite different. As a convenience to the miner and his family, credit was extended by issuing orders on the store in the form of scrip.[7]

Scrip was actually small tokens or coins with the company's name engraved upon them, that could be used instead of money to purchase items at the company store. The company could issue scrip to individual workers before pay day when they ran short of money. The cost of the scrip would then be deducted from the worker's next paycheck. For example, one dollar's worth of scrip might have the purchasing power of ninety cents at the company store. If the worker needed a ninety-cent scrip coin, the company issued him the scrip, and then deducted one dollar from his next paycheck.

It is maintained by coal operators that most company stores did not abuse the practice of issuing scrip, did not exploit the miners, and in fact operated on a profit margin considerably below that of most "private" stores in the area. They insist that most store operators were quite honest, although there were a few exceptions to this general rule which created a black eye for the whole industry. The rationale offered is that it certainly was not the fault of the company store that individual miners, through their own careless buying habits, became indebted to the store.

Another need that resulted from the isolation of the early coal towns, was the establishment of local public institutions, such as schools and churches. As an example, if the county had no schools within easy access to those who lived in the coal camp, the company would build a school at company expense, and would sometimes hire a teacher for the school until the time when the county school board could include the coal camp school in its budget. Even then, the company often supplemented the education of the children with additional school programs. "Many coal companies built churches and school buildings at each mining camp, and often supplemented the five or six months of schooling furnished by the county with an additional two or three months."[8]

The company usually built a coal camp church and subsidized the local preacher's salary so that the church could afford a full-time pastor. The companies often hired doctors for their workers and provided recreational facilities and events for the enjoyment of all the families in the community.

In most of these early coal camps, there was little or no provision for law enforcement from the county. Therefore, the coal companies soon began providing this service.

Usually in each coal town the company would appoint one employee as deputy sheriff whose job it was to maintain peace in the local community.

To preserve some semblance of order in the camps and on the branch line passenger trains, deputy sheriffs were employed. These men were deputized by the county sheriff but paid by the coal operators since the counties were not financially able to assume such a burden.[9]

According to the companies, these early mining towns were rough places and crime would undoubtedly have become rampant had not the company provided for the need of law enforcement.

This in general is how the coal companies viewed the structure of the coal camps. The company, by necessity, provided homes for the workers and established and maintained all institutions that were necessary for a community.

The Company Town as Gesellschaft

What began in theory as a planned community with a comprehensive program of services to miners, quickly developed into a complex system of controls. The coal camp became a closed society in which the entire life of the individual mining family became dependent upon and controlled by the company. The houses were built and owned by the company, and usually the workers were required to live in company housing. The company store was the only convenient place available to shop, and the scrip system of credit eventually placed most of the workers in perennial bondage to the company.

The schools were built by the company and the teachers were often on the company payroll in the early years. The police were company employees, and part of their job was to prevent unionization attempts. The churches were built and owned by the company and the local preachers were sometimes employees of the company. Most of the company-owned towns were not allowed to incorporate.

In short, the company towns that emerged in Appalachia were rationally planned towns, with a complex system of controls, that totally changed the structure of life in the area.

Returning to the definition of community in chapter two, it can be said that the company town of rural Appalachia by the early 1900s became the embodiment of

Tonnes's concept of Gesellschaft, and Weber's associative community.

First, the company town was a rationally planned unit that was based not upon relationship, but production. The entire focus of the town was oriented toward the economic end of producing coal or lumber. The traditional relationally based community life was undercut and redirected toward this end.

Traditional mores and authority were replaced by the careful manipulation of political power at the county and state levels. Enforcement of company policy was ensured by company police locally, and the workers lived and worked for the safe purpose of industrial production.

Bureaucratic rules and regulations emerged as the way of life in industrial towns. This was true at the local, county, and state level. The company made, interpreted, and enforced its bureaucratic mandates. Society was carefully and rationally planned structured and administered.

A vertical social structure emerged. Status and role became totally related to occupation and wealth. Social status and stratification was even reinforced geographically within most industrial towns, with the workers living in one area, the lower levels of management in larger homes in another area, and the company owner residing in the largest house, high on the hillside overlooking the town.

Personal and organizational alienation became a way of life. Division and competition were encouraged at all levels as a means of preventing unionization. Workers became alienated from company, from job, from one another.

Religion, instead of being the center of community, was transformed into an instrument of social stratification and political and economic manipulation. The one tie with former community life that remained fairly much intact, was kinship. Throughout the period of industrialization in Appalachia kinship ties remained strong.

Chapter Four Notes

1. Harry Caudill, *Night Comes to the Cumberlands* (Boston: Little, Brown and Company, 1963), p. 13.

2. Ibid., p. 72.

3. Oscar Deane Lambert, *Stephen Benton Elkins* (Pittsburgh: University of Pittsburgh Press, 1955), p. 54.

4. W. P. Tams, Jr., *The Smokeless Coal Fields of West Virginia* (Parsons, W.Va.: McClain Printing Company, 1963), p. 25.

5. Howard B. Lee, *Bloodletting in Appalachia* (Parsons, W.Va.: McClain Printing Company, 1964), p. 9.

6. Op. Cit., Caudill, p. 98.

7. Op. Cit., Tams, Jr., p. 52.

8. Ibid., p. 52.

9. Ibid., p. 59.

The Effect of Industrialization Upon Religion

Up to this point we have only briefly touched upon the nature of religious life in industrialized Appalachia. It now becomes necessary to examine in more depth exactly what effect this industrialization had upon the life of the church.

Theological Accommodations

The starting point for discussing the drastic changes undergone by religion in Appalachia during and after the industrialization of the area, is that of theological accommodation. There had to be some basic modification in religious thinking before such drastic changes could occur. Initially these changes occurred in two areas.

First was a great corruption in the Calvinistic work ethic. Calvinism did have several emphases that helped to lay the basis for the later development of capitalism. Calvinism certainly didn't create the rise of capitalism. But it did offer a philosophical background that gradually adapted itself to capitalism.

The strong emphases upon individualism, election, and hard work to the glory of God, accompanied by the concept that acquisition of wealth was not necessarily evil, were important ideological developments that were later corrupted and used to support the rapid industrial developments of the capitalists in America. By the late 1800s and early 1900s this had developed into a religion for industrialists based loosely on Calvinistic principles. In the 1930s H. Richard Niebuhr gave a burning indictment of this development of American capitalistic Christianity in his book *The Church Against the World.* In it Niebuhr states:

> The church is in bondage to capitalism. Capitalism in its contemporary form is more than a system of ownership and distribution of economic goods. It is a faith and a way of life. It is a faith in wealth as the source of all life's blessings and as the savior of man from his deepest misery. It is the doctrine that man's most important activity is the production of economic goods and that all other things are dependent upon this. On the basis of this initial idolatry it develops a morality in which economic worth becomes the standard by which to measure all other values and the economic virtues take precedence over courage, temperance, wisdom and justice, over charity, humility and fidelity. Hence nature, love, life, truth, beauty and justice are exploited or made the servants of the high economic good. Everything, including the lives of workers, is made a utility, is desecrated and ultimately destroyed. Capitalism develops a discipline of its own but in the long run makes for the overthrow of all discipline since the service of its goods demands the encouragement of unlimited desire for that which promises—but must fail—to satisfy the lust of the flesh and the pride of life.

> The capitalist faith is not a disembodied spirit. It expresses itself in laws and social habits and transforms the whole of civilization. It fashions society into an economic organization in which production for profit becomes the central enterprize, in which the economic relations of men are regarded as their fundamental relations, in which economic privileges are most highly prized, and in which the resultant classes of men are set to struggle with one another for the economic good. Education and government are brought under the sway of the faith. The family itself is modified by it. The structure of cities and the very architecture is influenced by the religion. So intimate is the relation between the civilization and the faith, that it is difficult to

42

participate in the former without consenting to the latter and becoming entangled in its destructive morality.[1]

This statement by Niebuhr is a comprehensive portrait of the effect that industrialization had upon religious thinking in America.

The relationship between Calvinism and the development of capitalism into an economic faith has often been denied. But when looking at the development of religion in Appalachia after the advent of industrialization, several facts are clear.

First, a large percentage of the industrialists who gained control of the land, built the railroads, leased their land for lumber and coal rights and made a fortune from the resources of Appalachia, as well as a high percentage of the mine and lumber mill operators, were Presbyterian. If not, they were certainly influenced by Calvinism and espoused a strong rationalistic work ethic. Oftentimes they were not active in the life of any church congregation, but gave strong financial support to religious institutions.

Secondly, in almost all of the company towns constructed, at least two churches were built. One was of the denomination of the owner, and a second was built of a competing denomination. More will be said about this at a later point.

In reading the philosophy of some of these industrialists, they did often seem to equate wealth, status, and power either as signs of God's grace, or at least as matter of destiny.

Finally, religion was oftentimes used as a rationalization for the development of capitalism. In fact, the condition of worker exploitation could easily be explained away by an appeal to individual initiative, coupled with a generally low view of the mass of humanity.

As a case in point, Henry G. Davis and Stephen B.

43

Elkins, of whom we have spoken earlier, were both Presbyterian in background. In every company town that Davis built, there was a Presbyterian Church established. Neither were very active in any church congregation, but both contributed large sums of money periodically as private acts of philanthropy. They both were strongly individualistic, and their manner of life attested to the fact that they believed that they were destined to acquire wealth and power.

The second theological accommodation that also influenced the capitalists and helped precipitate the major religious upheaval in Appalachia was liberalism and modernism. An outgrowth of rationalistic Calvinism, it emerged in the late 1800s as the result of scientific studies related to religion and was epitomized by the development of Biblical criticism. It eventually gave rise to controversies on the theory of evolution, biblical miracles and myths, and the general authority of the Bible. One result was the development of naturalistic religion based upon humanism epitomized by the Unitarian church.

A speech that caused a great furor among orthodox Christians was made by Charles A. Briggs when he was inducted as Edward Robinson, professor of biblical theology at Union Theological Seminary (New York) in 1891. It serves as a good example of a defense of modern scholarship. Briggs stated that there were several prevalent beliefs that served as obstructions to a sound view of the Bible. He enumerated them as superstition, verbal inspiration, authenticity, inerrancy, violation of the laws of nature, and minute prediction. In conclusion he stated:

> We have passed through these barriers that men have thrown up in front of the Word of God, the breastworks against Philosophy, History and Science. It is not surprising that multitudes of the best men of our age have rejected a Bible thus

44

guarded and defended, as if it could not sustain the light of day. Doubtless there are many who are thinking that the critics are destroying the Bible. They have so identified these outworks with the Bible itself that their Bible vanishes with these barriers. I feel deeply for them. . . . But I feel more deeply for those many men, honest and true, whom they have been keeping away from the Bible. I would say to all such: We have undermined the breastworks of traditionalism; let us blow them to atoms. We have forced our way through the obstructions; let us remove them from the face of the earth, that no man hereafter may be kept from the Bible, but that all may freely enter in, search it through and through, and find God enthroned in its very center.[2]

The development of modernism threatened the traditional structure of Christian theology throughout the Western world. And its shockwave was strongly felt in Appalachia.

It is likewise true that many of the industrialists were influenced by modern scientific and rationalistic understandings of religion. As an example, Festus P. Summers in his biography of Johnson Newlon Camden, a nineteenth century West Virginia industrialist, depicts this capitalist's religious philosophy:

Although a member of the Protestant Episcopal Church, his religious views showed but few of the influences of creed. His religious philosophy was in truth evolved from both rational, mundane experience and biblical interpretation. The by-product was kin to eighteenth century Deism. "I do not agree with the idea so common to laying most of our troubles upon the Lord," he wrote in 1902. "The Lord did not ordain our lives and in my judgement has very little to do in bringing us into this world or taking us out of it. All the universe is governed by laws fixed at its creation. Whenever we violate these laws we bring upon ourselves the penalty . . ." While he was a conformist, Camden deprecated the enervating influence of creed in the governance and practical operation of Christian churches. "The truth is that the religious sects have given a too literal and too narrow interpretation to the teachings of Christianity," he declared, "and in that way, in some instances, discredited the broad charity and benevolence of the Almighty and depicted His attributes in a manner repugnant to our sense of justice and divine law." In practice, however, he was a staunch supporter of the sects; and the latter leaned heavily upon him.[3]

Much more could be said. However, for our present purposes we need only to bear in mind that a corrupted capitalistic Calvinism, accompanied by the development of rationalistic liberalism and modernism, served as the theological and philosophical foundation for the religious upheaval that accompanied the industrialization of Appalachia.

The Compartmentalization of Religion

The second major factor that provided the basis for dramatic change in the nature and structure of religion, was the compartmentalization of religion. Prior to industrialization, religion generally penetrated all spheres of life. With the advent of industrialism the influence of religion was greatly reduced and narrowed into the "spiritual" realm. Economics, physical science, the social sciences, and medicine all became specialized fields of study in the late nineteenth century. In like manner religion became regarded as a specialized field that affected only one small segment of an individual's life or society as a whole.

Protestantism (by the time of the industrial revolution) largely accepted the compartmentalizing and secularizing of life which had been initiated by the Renaissance and which had been given special character in America by the separation of church and state. The heritage from later Puritanism, from the frontier and from revivalism had made protestants of the late nineteenth century individualistic to an unusual degree at the very moment when a corporate approach to the emerging industrial problems was needed. The doctrine of the church and the conception of the solidarity of society, both of which would have had great value in the social crisis, had suffered serious

46

erosion in the American environment. In some quarters, Protestantism had lost its dynamism and ethical vitality and, in scholastic fashion, thought of Christian truth as consisting of propositional statements.[4]

Even the dynamics of revivalism had been corrupted and weakened by the time of industrialization. Although always having an individualistic focus, until this point in American history it had also placed an emphasis upon social concern and care for one's neighbor. The religious awakenings of previous eras not only resulted in many personal conversions, they were also accompanied by social reforms and a general strengthening of the religious and ethical life of the community.

With the advent of industrialization, revivalism continued to be an important force in religious life, but the conversion experience became an end in itself. Conversion was weakened to imply a soft Christian piety for the individual, with no radical Christian demand for a change in society as a whole.

As Franklin Littell points out:

> Early revivalism had not hesitated to deal with major issues in society, had proclaimed the Lordship of Jesus Christ over all of life, had called upon men to repent, convert and be healed. In the latter half of the nineteenth century, various professional evangelists introduced a new style of message; avoiding any offenses to the ruling elements in the cities, their patrons, they concentrated on the "sins" of the workingmen: drinking, swearing, gambling, and joining unions.[5]

This generally weakened condition of religion throughout American society is vividly portrayed in Robert and Helen Lynd's study of *Middletown. Middletown* is the study of the changes that occurred in a midwestern community when it became industrialized. It gives us some interesting insights into the decline in the importance of religion.

First, there was a general change in the nature of

Christian beliefs. There was little belief system as such and an extremely wide variety of religious understandings. Faith was equated with "beliefs in the supremacy of Christianity, of the Bible, of God, and Jesus Christ, and in existence after death all touching what is called 'doctrine,' combined with at least a nominal belief in practical ethics, 'loving one's neighbor as oneself,' [and] a belief in the institution through which these religious habits of thought are taught."[6]

In addition, religion increasingly became less important among the working men of the community, and attendance at worship among both sexes declined considerably. "A check of attendance at the services of the forty-two religious bodies during the four-week period of October 26 to November 22, 1924, shows that an average of only eleven males in each 100 of white male population and eighteen females in each 100 of white female population attended Sunday morning services on each of the four Sundays."[7]

The function of traditional pastoral duties became narrowed and less important, and there was an increased activity among ministers in speaking engagements at clubs and social groups. There was, at the same time, a growing reticence among the male members of the community to honestly share their concerns with pastors.

From both ministers and their congregations an outsider gets an impression of the ministers as eagerly lingering about the fringes of things to get a chance to talk to the men of the city who in turn are diffident about frankly talking to them. On the one hand more than one man explained, as did a member of Rotary, "I'm afraid to talk to a preacher and tell him what I really think because he'd think me an athiest or something like that," and on the other hand one of the keenest ministers lamented to a staff member regarding the business men of the town whom he was desperately anxious to get closer to, "They'll talk to you, but they won't talk to me because I'm a minister and its the same with all the other ministers in town."[8]

In every aspect of the study, after industrialization the influence of religion narrowed greatly and its chief function appeared to be sort of a nominal spiritual undergirding for the status quo.

Doing Vs. Being

The Calvinistic work ethic came to full flower with the industrial revolution. True, there was a corruption of Calvin's original theological understandings. But the fact is that for Calvinists of the nineteenth century, work and doing was an important sign of God's grace. This concept became totally transferred to the understanding of the nature and purpose of the church.

It was with the emergence of the industrial revolution that organizational program began to be regarded as the most important function of the church. The church was viewed as an organization that needed to be structured for efficient programming. The precept became accepted that the individual congregation needed to organize itself in order to be able to minister effectively. Churches had to be structured in such a way that they could effectively plan and implement programs in worship, Sunday school, visitation, fellowship, growth and social ministry. A congregation was a good and viable church if it could effectively carry out these program areas.

This concept has continued to be emphasized throughout the past century in the major Protestant denominations. Accompanying this was the emphasis on membership and budget size. A church must be growing if it was a "good" church. In short, churches were evaluated by production standards much like any business or industry. This development was totally foreign to the experience of rural congregations. The rural church was the center of community life. But that was primarily a state of being. The church existed to undergird community life. A congregation did not have to plan programs for this to happen. The church was to be. It existed for fellowship and relationships.

The emphasis upon growth was not very strong either. After all, there was only a limited number of people. There was great rejoicing when a sinner was saved, but the joy was focused upon his salvation, not upon the bigger size of the church. The church was not viewed as an organization or institution, so much as a living organism.

These two concepts of the nature of the church were in direct opposition. Eventually, the view of the church as an efficient organization became accepted by most denominations as the standard for measuring success in ministry. Churches began to possess status depending upon their size and programs. This meant that small, rural churches were immediately reduced to lower status because they were small, poorly organized, and incapable of "doing" ministry effectively. Small congregations continuously had to try and rationalize the validity of their own existence to denominational leaders. This eventually resulted in the "image problem" that has plagued small, rural congregations for the past century.

Denominationalism

The final factor that accompanied industrialization and resulted in the transformation of the nature of religion in rural Appalachia was the growth of denominationalism. From the advent of the Reformation, new denominations had continuously been formed in Protestantism along the lines of theological doctrine. But there were, at the same time, great avenues of denominational cooperation, especially as the frontier church developed in rural Appalachia. It is also true that in early American town society, communities generally grew up around a single church or denomination.

It was not until the coming of industrialization that denominationalism along class lines became entrenched within individual communities. What is also interesting is that denominational entrenchment had little to do with doctrinal differences. Rather it was more often related to the adoption of the capitalistic values of money, growth, and status.

In the Middletown study to which we have previously referred, by 1920 there were forty-two church congregations in that city representing twenty-eight denominations. Traditional denominational differences had little effect, however. Most people generally believed about the same thing, and there was vast tolerance of religious beliefs in general.

And yet according to the testimony of people who have lived in Middletown during the entire period under study, there is more subtle church rivalry today than formerly, as financial and social competition, particularly among the business class, have tended to replace earlier doctrinal differences as lines of cleavage. The interdenominational mingling of an earlier day has apparently declined somewhat with the growth and differentiation of the community, competitive building programs, and national denominational financial burdens. As one housewife remarked, "When I was a girl here in Middletown people used to go about to the Christmas entertainments and other special services at the Methodist, Presbyterian, and other churches. People rarely do that sort of thing today." In the diary of a Middletown merchant one reads for the year 1890, "The new Christian Church dedicated today. No service at the Methodist or Baptist churches on account of it." "No service at our church (Presbyterian) on account of the dedication of the new Baptist church." And later still in 1890, "No service at our church—dedication of the Lutheran church." The competitive spirit made itself felt in the church of the writer of this diary under the stimulus of these new churches being built by other denominations and the local press in 1890 records: "Rev. G. A. Little preached a boom sermon at the Presbyterian church yesterday, presenting strong grounds in favor of building a new church. He predicted that in five years the Presbyterian church

would occupy the position the Presbyterian church in A——
does now and the size of our city would compare with (this same
neighboring city)." And sure enough, in 1894 the Presbyterians
outdid all the other new buildings by building the first cut stone
church in the city.[9]

Middletown was no isolated case. The fact is that with
industrialization, denominational competition hardened
along class lines, and eventually a whole new series of
sects and churches were born that helped to change the
nature of religion throughout Appalachia.

The Nature of Religion in the Company Town

We have previously discussed in some detail the structure of company town society that emerged with the industrialization of Appalachia. The company town church
fit neatly into this overall system of control.

The company built the churches within each town, and
their financial support to a great degree continued to be
dependent upon the company. As late as 1950 after
unionization had occurred and the company town structure generally collapsed, a survey of coal camp churches
in West Virginia showed that of the thirty-nine churches
responding, seventeen were directly owned by the company.[10] It was in the interest of the company, of course,
to ensure that these religious institutions would not
become the source of any turmoil or discord.

Partially by design and partially growing out of the
Appalachian religious heritage, the church of the coal
camp was usually other-worldly oriented in its theology,
with little practical hope for the present life problems
confronting the workers.

An atmosphere of other-worldliness is quite common . . .
hymns and songs are replete with references to heaven. . . . The
Gospel is usually preached in personal terms, and within rather
narrow limits. One receives the impression that here are gen-
uinely devout and good people aiming to live good Christian

52

lives within the accepted mores and within their immediate area of personal association, with little awareness of the implications of their faith in the larger circles of human associates.[11]

The rather weak ethical moralism that resulted from the compartmentalization of religion usually entailed a strong individualistic work ethic that was generally supportive of the economic structure of coal camp life. We have previously seen the change in revivalism away from any social dynamic and toward a watered down pietism that accompanied industrialization. This certainly was characteristic of coal camp revivals, and preaching focused upon moralistic judgements directed toward the working man.

The theological mindset of these rural industrial towns in Appalachia, created a strong reaction against the trends toward modernism and liberalism. We can be assured that there would have been general agreement in most company towns with this sermon excerpt recorded in *Middletown:*

> We are in the midst of a period of criticism in which certain so-called "intellectuals" are trying to destroy the Bible and men's faith in the fundamentals of Christianity, but the Bible still stands. . . . The Bible comes from God and is the divine authority and His revelation to men. No great piece of oratory or literature can come from any other fountainhead. There could have been no Patrick Henry, Abraham Lincoln, Wendell Phillips, or Daniel Webster without it. . . . These may be dark days but there have been others in history. . . . In the darkest hour of human history (Jesus Christ) is coming back again. When He comes the world will have a King that is above every other king and who swings the scepter of peace and rules the nations of the earth.[12]

Denominational competition became strongly entrenched within coal camp society. When the company towns were constructed, more than one church was always built regardless of the size of the town. The churches usually developed along class lines with one church being a management congregation, and one or two churches being working class congregations.

Liston Pope in his classic study of religion in the mill towns of Gaston County, North Carolina, carefully documents the phenomena of denominationalism along class lines in that area. The same type of thing developed in the coal and lumber towns of Appalachia.

At the same time, church competition became one means of preventing unionization. In one small coal town of Randolph County, West Virginia, the workers went on strike about 1898. There was but one church in the town at that time. The mine owner sold the mine to Henry G. Davis who promptly broke the strike by importing immigrant Italian laborers. He built a Roman Catholic Church for the Italian workers, and that town has remained deeply divided along denominational lines to the present day. The same tactic was used over and over again in company towns all over the region. So the church, instead of being a unifying and socially integrative force within community life, became a divisive force that fortified and strengthened class prejudices.

The company town preacher, far from being a strong social and moral influence within the community, was usually instead a company employee. The minister was often on the payroll of the company and the church was so heavily financially indebted to the company that there was seldom any chance that a minister would speak or act in any way against the structure of coal camp life.

Again, the 1950 study showed that even at that late date, ten of thirty preachers of the coal camp churches surveyed, were on the direct payroll of a coal company.[13]

> If a minister should become involved with a passion for social justice, it is doubtful if he could remain in a company owned parish. . . . The church in the company-owned community, therefore, tends to be part of a system of control rather than to be a constant challenge to greater social justice.[14]

54

The complicity of company preachers in the system of coal camp controls is again borne out by Pope's study of mill town religion. His analysis was that:

> There have been no public statements or discernible private pressures from ministers or local ecclesiastical bodies concerning regulation of wages and hours, changes in working conditions, public accountability of mill managements, distribution of profits, or any comparable question. Structurally controlled by the mills and culturally conditioned by traditions and attitudes that sanction the industry without qualification, the churches and their representatives have been in no position or mood to criticize or to render unfavorable appraisal. Institutional pressures from churches on the mills simply have not existed, so far as any question of importance is concerned.[15]

Worship in the coal camp churches reflected the theology of the churches and was other-worldly directed with little relevance for practical living. Emphasis upon the Second Coming of Jesus was very strong, with no direct appeal for changing the present social order. Revivalism was strong, but again the emphasis was totally upon the individual conversion experience, and pietistic moralisms aimed at the working man.

The church was strictly antiunion in its approach. Pope's study of the mill town churches showed that in the unionization attempts undertaken by Communists in the 1930s the churches aligned strongly on the side of management against the workers. The company preachers used the pulpit as a media for berating their parishioners about the threat of godless Communism, and most condoned the use of mob violence against the union organizers. There was never any mention made of the working conditions that had precipitated these unionization efforts. And the preacher's opposition to the strike had little to do with their financial tie to the company.

Most of the ministers, nevertheless, appear to have been sincerely opposed to the strike apart from questions of personal advantage. They were constrained by general culture much more powerfully than they could have been by fear or financial self-interest. They shared the general presuppositions of the community as to proper industrial relations. They endorsed, as they still do the tradition that the mills represent a blessing without qualification, and therefore should be carefully protected, and that mill workers should look up to their employers in gratitude and patience. If an individual were not satisfied, they believed he should seek to better his lot through individual action; a strike never does any good and causes trouble for everybody. That mill workers should be willing to follow Communists proves that they are children, easily misled, who must be cared for. It stands to reason that the employer, living in the same community with the workers, knows better how to take care of them than these "outside agitators" who are after their money, and who are teaching them all sorts of doctrines that run diametrically contrary to the Christian religion.[16]

The coal camp churches aligned against unionization attempts in the early 1900s in Appalachia, in much the same manner as did the company town churches of Gaston County. Religion in industrialized Appalachia then, far from serving the socially integrative functions it once had, became a divisive force within the coal camp culture and in all too many instances an oppressive arm of control used by management against the workers.

Colonialism, the Missionary Mentality, and the Cultural Assimilation of the Natives

Appalachia stands in the tradition of colonialism. Colonialism as we have come to know it is a fairly recent phenomena in the history of mankind, and rose to prominence as the established economic practice of Western European nations by the late sixteenth century.

Originally colonialism was directly related to the economic mercantile theories and the desire of the European powers to build up reserves of so-called precious metals. In order to accomplish this, exports had to exceed imports.

Climatic conditions and lack of natural resources prevented nations such as Great Britain from being able to meet all their economic needs. Therefore, it was desirable to establish colonies throughout the world to produce for the mother country those products which otherwise would have to be purchased from other nations.

English colonization was primarily carried out by private corporations known as joint-stock companies. These companies invested in the establishment of specific colonies, and derived the economic profit from the goods produced in those colonies. It is this English tradition of colonialism that has most influenced American colonialism.

There are a number of characteristics of colonialism. First, colonialism is carried out by private companies for economic profit with the full sanction and support of the government.

Secondly, colonialism is an economically extractive enterprise, in which the aim is to extract natural resources from the colony at as little cost as is possible. In order to do this, control of the land and resources must be established.

Next, professional representatives from the corporation are sent into the colonized area to oversee the operation. They usually establish colonial towns where they live, as their base of operations. Often cheap native labor is employed, or foreign labor is imported, to extract the needed resources. Political control of the area is established through the colonial towns.

A cultural superiority is assumed by the colonizing nation, and an intentional attempt of the cultural assimilation of the native peoples is often attempted. In many cases this results in revolution.

Finally, religious missionary enterprises have always

gone hand in hand with colonization, and religion often becomes the principal means of cultural assimilation. This assimilation via religion we shall term the "missionary mentality." It assumes a cultural superiority, and its focus is not only on evangelizing the natives but also on changing their lifestyle and values.

The great foreign missionary movement of the nineteenth century into Africa occurred simultaneously with the colonization of that continent. In the process of establishing schools, churches, and hospitals to help the natives, in many cases the indigenous culture was totally destroyed.

In almost every respect much of Appalachia became an economic colony of the northeastern industrialists following the Civil War. And it is likewise true that the company town churches became the means by which some of the major denominations carried out their home mission enterprises in this colonized area. This missionary zeal went hand in hand with the theme of Manifest Destiny which became popularized during this era of industrial and colonial expansion.

In this period of expansion, many churchmen tried to give theological expression to the concept of American destiny. The early New England Puritans had seen their theocracies as God's new Israel, a "wilderness Zion," which occupied a central place in God's plan for mankind. In the era of the Revolution the theme had been renewed and brought up-to-date by patriotic clergymen. God, they then said, was bringing to birth a new nation to serve him. The idea was further developed during the nineteenth century. Perry Miller has suggested that between the Revolution and the Civil War the old ideal of a covenanted nation was replaced by the ideal of individual Christians and voluntaristic churches dedicated to the national purpose, religiously conceived. God was expanding American power because the "Anglo-Saxons" were his chosen agents to bring blessings to the world.[17]

Following the Civil War this emphasis upon American destiny was renewed among the clergy. This gave impetus to a new missionary zeal around the world that not only entailed converting the pagan peoples, but also alleviation of social needs, which at times included the acculturation of whole societies of people.

It was at this point that the cultural captivity of American Christianity became complete and the American economic system began to be equated with Christian principles. As H. Richard Neibuhr has pointed out: "The building of the Kingdom of God has been confused in many a churchly pronouncement with the increase of church possessions or with the economic advancement of mankind. The church has often behaved as though the saving of civilization and particularly of capitalist civilization were its mission."[18]

The point is that in Appalachia this type of missionary enterprise was undertaken. And the company town church often became the institution through which attempts at assimilation were carried out.

From the standpoint of the emerging industrialized culture of America, the people of the Appalachian mountains were considered a bit strange for wanting to live in that mountain wilderness area. It was, of course, natural for those who came into the region, to assume a cultural superiority. It therefore became part of the mission of the company town church to "change the people" to better fit into an industrialized society.

Fundamentalism as a Reaction

The final development that had an extensive influence upon the nature and function of religion in West Virginia after industrialization was fundamentalism. Fundamentalism accompanied the growth of industrialization throughout the nation. It began first in the urban areas, but spread quickly to the rural areas as well.

Fundamentalism initially emerged as a reaction against the modernist-liberal trends in theology. Its founder was Lyman Stewart, an oil millionaire, who re-affirmed in 1909 what he termed the seven fundamentals of the Christian faith. They were as follows: (1) The verbal inspiration of the Bible as originally given, (2) The deity of Christ, (3) The vicarious death of Jesus, (4) The personality of the Holy Spirit, (5) The necessity of a personal infilling of the Spirit for victorious Christian living, (6) The personal return of Christ, (7) The urgency of speedy evangelization of the world.[19]

> As is true of most creeds, this one was fashioned as an apologetic weapon and reflects the stress being placed upon Christian dogma at certain critical points. Thus the first three articles mirror one troubled Christian's attempt to reaffirm doctrines being questioned by Liberal theologians. The last four articles, however, reflect not the attacks of the Modernists but the favorite themes of the millenarian movement. Points four and five seem to reflect Keswick doctrines of personal holiness, the sixth the premillennial advent of Christ, and point seven the missionary concerns. . . .[20]

Fundamentalism quickly became a strong movement that eventually gave rise to numerous new sectarian groups. It was characterized by emotionalism, and a strong emphasis upon Biblical literalism and the eminent return of Jesus. It had a major attraction for the lower social and economic classes and it filled the void left by the major denominations with their weakened culturalized religion.

In essence, fundamentalism grew to be not only a reaction against modernism, but also a reaction against modern industrialized society in general. It became the faith of the social and economic outcasts of society, and a theological haven for those whose values and belief system had been threatened by industrialized society.

Fundamentalism quickly became an important force in

the religious life of Appalachia. It came into being at the exact time that the union organizing wars were beginning in the coalfields. With the abandonment of the working men by the company town denominational churches, sectarian churches quickly began to grow up in the rural areas outside the towns. They emerged initially as an option to the totally culturalized religion of the company towns, and quickly began to attract the working class of people.

The fundamentalist sectarian churches of Appalachia never offered the same type of foundation for social protest as did the black churches of the South. But they did emerge fairly free of company control and offered something of a religious haven for the oppressed. They became the embodiment of the indigenous mountain culture and religion. In short, the so-called sect churches became the norm.

These fundamentalist sectarian churches were antimodernist, anti-upper class, anticompany, and anti-this world. In every way fundamentalism in Appalachia became a moral and theological reaction against the controlled society that had been superimposed on Appalachia by the industrialization of the region.

The Cycle of Paternalistic Control and Abandonment

The history of denominational support of the small churches in rural Appalachia has been typified by a recurring cycle of paternalistic control and periodic abandonment. The cycle of paternalism and abandonment has coincided directly with the boom and bust economy of the region.

Each period of economic boom in the region has been accompanied by a renewal of interest and support by denominational judicatories. There is strong economic and vocal support given to existing churches. In addition,

61

during each of these eras new churches are started. Through this process of renewed interest and support, close control and supervision has normally been exercised over these small churches by the judicatories.

But during periods of economic collapse the interest and support of these same denominational judicatories has often waned and been withdrawn. During these periods of turmoil and economic depression, when the support and stability of some community institution is most needed, these small rural churches have often either been closed, or abandoned to make it on their own.

This cycle of paternalism and abandonment quite naturally heightened the level of mistrust of the laity of small churches, against the denominational judicatory. And this was perhaps the most devastating long-range effect of industrialization upon the small rural churches of Appalachia.

The Loss of Identity of the Small Church

The small, rural church was transformed and weakened through this complex process of social and cultural change that accompanied the industrialization of the region.

Most such congregations that had existed before the advent of industrialization became lost and in a state of decline amid the condition of social stratification and denominational competition. They became increasingly alienated from the growing denominational bureaucratic structure, with its increased emphasis upon program and congregational size.

They suddenly discovered that they were existing apart from the norm of organized religion in the area. Such congregations could not fully identify themselves with the sectarian churches, but they were heavily influenced by the theology and structure of these emerging indigenous congregations.

In addition, through becoming captured by and identified with the control of industrial town society, these small churches had become alienated from the common working man. Yet, they existed in a culture that was to be increasingly influenced by a growing and militant labor force. In many industrial towns of today, women are the mainstay of the church. Most of the men still refuse to identify in any way with church life.

The typical small denominational church in rural Appalachia suddenly found itself adrift on a sea of uncertainty, in search of a new identity, cut off from any real sense of mission, increasingly brought under criticism by both its denomination and the society around it, and competing in a life and death struggle for survival.

The Function of Religion in Appalachia Re-examined

With the advent of industrialization, religion no longer fulfilled any of the traditional socially integrative functions in Appalachia. Far from being the glue that solidified community, religion became but another social force that led to the destruction of the traditional horizontal social structure in rural communities.

First, there was no longer a unified belief system. There still remained a few vestiges of agreement on some of the essentials of the Christian faith, but religion became so individualized that there was no longer any emphasis upon community responsibility. The spectrum of belief in Appalachia swung between the totally culturalized religion of the coal camp church, and the antisocial theology of the fundamentalist sectarian churches.

Religion, then, no longer was a solidifying influence within the community. Rather, it was a source of division along denominational lines. Competition between churches was encouraged, and religion generally reinforced a vertical class structure.

63

In some ways the revivalistic religion did serve a re-energizing function for the individual. But it no longer really prepared the individual person to be a part of the community or to face the everyday trials of living, with hope. Rather it served as a form of escapism that left the individual isolated with only a futuristic hope in the Second Coming.

In no way did religion serve the traditional leveling function in society. Instead, it became a means of solidifying and reinforcing class differences and an heirarchical social structure based upon economic status. It reinforced the belief in individualism to the degree that there was a total disregard for the plight of the poor and social outcasts.

In summary, with the advent of industrialization, religion quickly evolved into a generally destructive force within the local community in Appalachia. In essence, it became a major part of the problem.

The charts on the following pages outline the major changes that occurred in community structure, and the basic function of religion in rural Appalachia, through the process of industrialization.

The Change in Community Structure

Traditional Community Structure	*Company Town Structure*
1. Community emerged naturally over many generations.	1. The town is carefully planned and built by the company.
2. Community is based upon kinship.	2. The town is based upon production and a hired labor force.
3. Horizontal social structure with a minimum drive for status by persons.	3. Vertical social structure in which status and social stratification is encouraged.

4. Ebb and flow to geographic boundaries of community
5. Economic and social life is based upon cooperation and reciprocity.
6. Economy is based upon barter.
7. Personal identity is found in the context of family/community.
8. Economic and social needs are met by family and community.
9. Social organization is based upon tradition and the elders of the family and community.
10. Wholistic approach to life. People do many things. Jack of all trades.
11. Time according to the rhythms of life . . . appropriate time.
12. Decision making is by concensus and based upon traditional authority.
13. History is stories and oral tradition.
14. Religion is the center of community . . . the undergirding, unifying

4. Fixed geographic boundaries for the town.
5. Economic and social life is based upon competition and social stratification.
6. Economy is based upon money.
7. Personal identity is based upon work. You are what you do.
8. Economic and social needs are met by the company.
9. Social organization is bureaucratized.

10. Specialization in work.

11. Highly scheduled time. Work is by shifts.
12. Decision making is based upon voting and political power.
13. History is analytical and based upon data.
14. Religion is a divisive force in community life and a means of social

force in community life. stratification. Religion is typified by denominationalism.

The Function of Religion in Community Life

Traditional Community Structure	The Church in the Company Town
1. The church is an indigenous expression of culture and community. The church building is constructed as a community effort.	1. The church is imposed by the company. The building is constructed, owned, and maintained by the company.
2. Support of the church and building is a cooperative community effort.	2. Financial support of the church is often imposed by the check-off.
3. The preacher is a missionary of the denomination sent in upon the request of the church, or is a local lay preacher. The preacher often serves a circuit. Primary responsibilities are preaching, revivals, and sacraments. Church decisions are made independent of the preacher.	3. The preacher is either an employee of the company, or a missionary sent in by the denomination at the company's request. The preacher becomes a controlling influence in the congregation.
4. One church building per town is the norm. There is one congregation that might have	4. Several competing churches and church buildings, usually along class lines.

affiliation with more than one denomination.

5. Unifying belief system—normally a combination of Calvinism and Methodism, adapted to mountain society.

6. Camp revival serves reenergizing function. People are renewed to live in community.

7. Community cyclical celebrations of birth, marriage, and death are through the community church.

8. Church enforces moral standards—excommunication meant exclusion from community.

9. Church undergirds indigenous culture.

10. Church is a means of redistribution of wealth.

5. No belief system— competing beliefs.

6. Revivals become more individualized. The church heightens the separation of the individual from community.

7. Cyclical celebrations become more individualized and secularized.

8. Religion deals more with moralisms . . . especially aimed at the sins of the working people.

9. Church, through missionaries, becomes a means of assimilation and change.

10. Compartmentalization of religion into the spiritual realm. Company/government takes function of redistribution of wealth.

| 11. Church provides level-ing influence. | 11. Church prevents level-ing. Reinforces social stratification. |
| 12. The church is an organism. | 12. The church is an organization. |

Admittedly the change from rural to industrialized society in Appalachia in the late 1800s and early 1900s, and its subsequent effect upon the small church there, is an extreme example. But it does, I think, offer a plausible explanation for the situation of many of the small churches in our society as a whole.

Our entire society has been greatly affected by the change from rural agrarianism to urban industrialization over the past century. Appalachia merely affords us a study of an area in which that change occurred more rapidly, and the subsequent social trauma was more acute and visible.

In other parts of America the changes have come more slowly perhaps, but have been just as far-reaching. And the fact remains that most of the small churches in our society, whether in urban areas or rural areas, still embody the values of that past agrarian based culture. This glimpse of the effect of industrialization upon the small church in Appalachia, does offer some general explanation for the state of many of the small churches in our society as a whole.

Chapter Five Notes

1. H. Shelton Smith, Robert T. Handy, and Lefferts A. Leetacher, *American Christianity—An Historical Interpretation With Representative Documents* (New York: Charles Scribner's Sons, 1960), vol. 2, p. 444.

2. Ibid., pp. 278-79.

3. Festus P. Summers, *Johnson Newlon Camden: A Study in Individualism* (Garden City, N.Y.: G. P. Putnam's Sons, 1937), p. 564.

4. Op. Cit., Smith, vol. 2, p. 360.

5. Franklin Hamlin Littell, *From State Church to Pluralism* (Garden City, N.Y.: Doubleday and Company, Inc., 1962), p. 125.

6. Robert S. Lynd, and Helen Merrell Lynd, *Middletown* (New York: Harcourt, Brace and World, Inc., 1956), p. 321.

7. Ibid., p. 358.

8. Ibid., p. 351.

9. Ibid., pp. 333-34.

10. Mark Rich, *Some Churches In Coal Mining Communities of West Virginia* (New York: West Virginia Council of Churches, 1951), p. 43.

11. Ibid., p. 40.

12. Op. Cit., Lynd, p. 377.

13. Op. Cit., Rich, p. 46.

14. Homer Lawrance Morris, *The Plight of the Bituminous Coal Miner* (Philadelphia: University of Pennsylvania Press, 1934), p. 93.

15. Liston Pope, *Millhands and Preachers* (New Haven: Yale University Press, 1967), pp. 202-3.

16. Ibid., p. 278.

17. Op. Cit., Smith, vol. 1, pp. 4-5.

18. Ibid., p. 445.

19. Ernest R. Sandeen, *The Roots of Fundamentalism* (Chicago: The University of Chicago Press, 1970), p. 192.

20. Ibid., p. 192.

CHAPTER SIX

Redefining the Church as the Center of Community

Having examined the historical foundations of the small church, we have now arrived at the point where we can begin to understand the unique purpose and mission of the small church today. For the central intent of this book is not to focus on what is wrong with the small church. Rather our interest is to envision what the church should become. And it is my contention that the small church could become the leaven for the rediscovery of community life.

Redefining Community for Today

If the remainder of this study is to focus on the re-emergence of the small church as the center of community, then it is first necessary to redefine what is meant by community. The definition of community that served as a theoretical basis for the preceding portion of the study related primarily to a preindustrial image of community typified by primitive society. The essence of community was kinship relationship, undergirded by religion, and focusing on meeting human needs.

For the most part, these same components can remain in a redefinition of community that is workable in modern industrialized society. This is particularly true

70

in rural areas. There are, however, a few different emphases that must be considered if community is to become a practical reality in our day and time.

First, the concept of community must move beyond the geographic limits of town. Community is dynamic and far transcends township limits. There is a natural ebb and flow to community boundaries, and today they are more psychological than geographic. There are points at which community can be as broadly defined as county, and other points when it is as narrow as family and friends.

Whatever the boundaries, however, there must be certain unifying factors that undergird relationships and create community. In general, for rural areas the traditional ties of culture, kinship, and tradition still form a base upon which community can be built. At the same time, considering the mobility of modern society which is increasingly affecting rural areas, community ties must begin to reach beyond these traditional limitations. It is in this connection that the emergence of a new concept of community is essential.

By a new concept of community I'm not referring to an antiurban, antiindustrial mindset, for this type of negativism is already present, and serves more to divide people than to provide any unifying force. What is needed is a new, positive understanding of what it means to be part of society in modern America. It includes a positive relationship with the land, and a reaffirmation of the centrality of personal friendship and neighborliness. It is, in essence, a reaffirmation of values that place persons above machines, and community above production. It is this type of concept that can facilitate the reemergence of community.

In a sense, then, community is an emerging theoretical concept that is in the process of becoming. Having said this, it is important to emphasize that the time has come for the concept of community to move beyond the theoretical stage, and be willfully and carefully planned.

One of the characteristics of modern society that both Tonnes and Weber recognized as differentiating it from past community life, was that the modern industrial town was intentionally planned and constructed. For them this was a negative factor. They felt that community must be grounded in natural human relationships. It could not be planned and constructed, and in any sense remain real.

I would question that thesis. I would maintain that it was not the planned, intentionality of industrial towns that was destructive, but the shift in emphasis away from the primary purpose of community as a relational entity. It was the functional and productive focus of industrial towns that undercut community life and relationships.

As a matter of a fact, I would maintain that, unless community is carefully planned and intentionally recreated in our modern society, it will never recur. Left to the natural forces of modern industrial life, any remaining sense of community will dissolve, and society will continue on its bureaucratic, spiral toward total depersonalized regimentation.

There are several inherent characteristics that must be included in the reemergence and recreation of community life. First is the dynamic interplay between relationship and function, being and doing.

The essential nature of former primitive communities was the fact that they were predicated upon relationship, but unconsciously focused on cooperative effort to meet group needs. The same must be true if community is to become a reality today.

The relational ties must be real. And as stated previously, the emergence of a new and positive concept of community can become the foundation of the mutual

72

identity necessary for creating this relational base. At the same time community will not become real until this relational base enables persons to live cooperatively to meet mutual needs.

The functional basis of community is not to be confused or identified with the production basis of the industrial town. The cooperative effort to meet need must move beyond the realm of economic production to include all levels of human need, material, spiritual, emotional, and aesthetic.

The third necessary component of community is that it must be judged by the standard of human justice. Community must not only be human, but also humane. The manipulation of political power and the acquiescence to a nonexistent traditional authority, must be replaced by a local politic aimed at human justice.

Finally, any modern community must become adaptive to change. Change of one form or another is inherent in modern life. Uncompromising resistance to change will not alter it. What can be affected is the form and nature of that change. Only through cooperative endeavor can people begin to direct the course of the inevitable change that will occur in their society. Only through cooperative living can change be planned for, so that it will enable life to be enriched, rather than destroyed.

If the preceding is a practical theoretical ideal, then community, as Buber maintains, must have a spiritual center. And it is at this point that the small church faces its greatest challenge.

The Church as the Center of Community

It is my assumption that the small church can emerge as the center and foundation of community. This is true whether or not all or even most of the people in a given town are directly related to a church. For what we are speaking of is not an organizational entity as such, but a sphere of concern and influence. And in that connection the small church can be reborn as the center of community life.

The key is to understand that the concept of community church is not a geographic reality, but a state of consciousness. The church, any church, is only as large, only as broad, only as important, as the consciousness of its members allows it to be.

There are at least three practical ways that the small church can become the center of community. The first is spiritually. Community must have a spiritual center. The small church can fulfill this void. The small church can become an instrument for spiritual community renewal, and the seedbed for the emergence of the new community consciousness that was mentioned earlier.

If members of small churches can begin to move beyond the survival mentality, and catch a vision of a new identity of being God's agents for the redemption of community, this can begin to occur. This spiritual identity is related directly to the need for developing a theology of life.

Secondly, the church can become the center of community in terms of emotional support. The small church has always fulfilled this need for its own members. But the need here is for the small church to learn how to move beyond its own bounds to offer care and support for those who are not related to the church. This is perhaps the most difficult task with which to deal.

Finally, the small church can become the center of life in a very functional and practical sense. In fact, the initial step that must be taken in order to lead the church beyond the survival syndrome is directly related to the use of the church building itself. The church building can become a center for community activity. When this begins to happen, the individual congregation immediately breaks through its traditional limitations of denominationalism, to become viewed as an essential part of community life.

As has been stated, the objective of this study is to demonstrate how some small churches can become revitalized and recapture this unique mission of undergirding community. Therefore, the second major part of this book will focus on the specific steps by which a small church can move from a survival mentality to a community based congregation.

Part Two

Revitalizing the
Small Church

CHAPTER SEVEN

The Developmental Stages in the Life of a Small Church

We have stated that the history of the small church in America has resulted in many small congregations losing sight of their unique mission of creating and undergirding community life. This loss of mission has resulted in many small churches becoming weak. This problem is interwoven with the fabric of congregational life. There is nothing wrong with the people. But they have learned a bitter lesson from history. That lesson is that their congregation may soon die.

This key problem is what I have termed the survival syndrome. For many of our smaller congregations, institutional survival has become their main reason for being. The roots of this survival syndrome as we have seen in past chapters, are deep and complex. It seems to manifest itself in the following ways.

The foundation of this survival syndrome is a basic identity crisis. People in many small churches sense that their church is out of step with other churches. They know that their church is different. They know that it is not successful. They know that the denominational judicatories consider them to be a problem.

This sense of feeling different and unsuccessful often produces an atmosphere of self-pity. They feel there is something wrong with them. They are not liked by the denomination. After all, the denominational judicatory is always speaking of the small church problem. They feel that they are not liked by their pastors, for most of their pastors leave after only two or three years. They often feel that they are not really liked by others in their own community, for new people seldom come to their church. If a new family does visit their congregation, oftentimes they do not come back. So members of many smaller congregations feel that something is wrong with them, for experience has taught them that this is so.

Growing out of this feeling of self pity is usually a feeling of weakness. They feel that they are incapable of doing much of anything very well. Programs that have been attempted by pastors in the past have often failed. They don't have anything much to offer new families that might come to their church. In short, they have grown to expect and be satisfied with mediocrity and failure.

Finally, there usually grows up a very honest fear for institutional survival. The membership of such small congregations is often static, or declining. Oftentimes most of the members are middle-aged or older. They know that with rising inflation they probably will never be able to afford their own pastor. Indeed, they may not even be able to afford to pay the current expenses of building upkeep. They have seen other small churches around them close. And they live in fear of the day when the church judicatory representatives will visit their congregation, and tell them that the church must close its doors and be dissolved.

Therefore, the chief aim and mission of the congregation is to survive. This survival syndrome becomes a vicious cycle, a way of life for the congregation. It seems to stand as an impenetrable wall.

Oftentimes, however, with careful work and planning, the situation can change. Many small congregations, even ones totally weighted down by the survival syndrome, can become revitalized. But this revitalization involves a process that takes time, careful planning, and hard work.

Five Stages in the Revitalization of a Small Church

There is a long-range process involved in the total revitalization of congregations that become trapped by the enigma of the survival syndrome. There are at least five natural developmental phases through which a congregation must move in order to become revitalized with a new sense of mission. And one of the key variables is having a pastor who is willing to stay long enough to enable the church to move through each phase. This process of revitalization normally takes five to seven years.

When speaking of the revitalization of small churches, the intent is not to assume that the task is aimed at creating large congregations with extensive programming. The objective is to help create vital, small congregations. The objective is to create congregations that are able to affirm themselves, that grow enough to ensure institutional survival, that discover their unique mission of undergirding community and that are equipped to plan and carry out the programs that the people of those congregations want to accomplish.

This process of revitalization begins with a phase of reaffirmation and rediscovery. This is the stage during which all of the positive aspects of congregational life are reaffirmed and celebrated.

It begins with the affirmation that there is nothing wrong with being small, that indeed part of the basic strength of the congregation is its small size. This involves affirming the basic strength and goodness of the quality of relationships within the congregation. It involves reaffirming that natural function of caring for one another, and perhaps even improving how that is done.

81

The phase of reaffirmation involves celebrating the history and tradition of the congregation. It could involve developing a printed history of the church, or setting aside special times of the year to celebrate the history and tradition of the church.

The entire phase of reaffirmation is directed toward affirming that the congregation is good, and indeed has some very basic strengths. It is aimed at enabling the members of the congregation to know that the mere fact that they are different and small is not bad, but is something to be celebrated and built upon.

The second stage in the process of revitalization is the stage of initial victories. This involves rediscovering how to plan and do some things well. It would involve planning one or two programs that the congregation really wants done, and then carrying them out to completion. Having this occur even once or twice can begin to reverse the cycle of defeatism.

This second stage is also the one during which the pastor begins to be trusted because he/she has not decided to move. It is during this time that the congregation discovers that the pastor enjoys being part of the life of their congregation.

This is also the stage during which one or two new families come into the church. Even the addition of one new family to a small church can be a major victory, and provide a tremendous emotional spiritual lift for the entire congregation.

The third stage is that of rediscovering identity. Once reaffirmation has occurred, and the congregation has begun to experience some successes, the entire membership of the church needs to become involved in a process of study to rediscover what their unique purpose and mission is.

This can include rediscovery of theology. The congregation might become involved in a six-month study of theology aimed at creating their own congregational statement of faith. This period of rediscovery might involve renewing their denominational ties. It might involve a study of worship, aimed at developing and building up their own expressions of worship. It might involve starting some new traditions within the church, or rediscovering their link with the community.

The fourth stage of revitalization is the stage of learning to plan programs effectively. Program planning in smaller churches usually fails for one of three reasons. Either it is done poorly, or it is done for and by the pastor, or the process does not take into account the basic relational nature of the church.

It is during this fourth stage that the congregation initiates a triennial planning process of goal setting, program planning, and program implementation, aimed at carrying out the specific programs that the congregation wants and needs to do. Also involved is a process of annual review and evaluation, and celebration of accomplishments.

The fifth and final stage in the revitalization of the small church is its reemergence as a community based congregation. This is the process of learning how the church can minister and relate to the community, and undergird community life.

These, then, are the developmental stages in the revitalization of the small church. And the key to the entire process is the pastor.

CHAPTER EIGHT

The Small Church Pastor

The key factor in a small church experiencing revitalization is the pastor. This does not mean that the entire
task of revitalization in the small church is dependent
upon the pastor doing everything. However, it is difficult to envision a small church experiencing revitalization without its pastor enabling this process to occur.

The pastor is extremely important to the life of a small
congregation. It is important to the laity that they feel
that their pastor likes them and cares for them. In fact,
the ability to perform ministerial functions capably is
probably not nearly as important to persons in small
churches, as is the willingness of the pastor to invest his
or her life in the lives of the people in the congregation.

The Pastor as the Problem

In many small churches, the pastor has often been
part of the problem, rather than part of the solution to
the revitalization process. For there have been three
basic types of pastors who have frequently served small
churches.

First are the ones who possess a retirement mentality.
This does not mean that older pastors are ineffective as
small church pastors. Quite the opposite is true. Probably the best pastors that many small churches have
had, have been older pastors with wisdom and ex-

perience, who still have the vision and vitality to work creatively with their congregation.

However, there are some older pastors who have been called to smaller churches as their last step before retirement. And these pastors have sometimes been possessed by a retirement mentality. They are burned out after thirty years of ministry, and are in no way equipped to lead a small congregation through a process of revitalization. It should be added, however, that those who possess the retirement mentality are much less destructive than the other two types of ministers who have often served small churches.

The second type of pastor who has frequently served the small church is the young pastor motivated by the stepping stone mentality. This is the pastor who is frequently in his or her first pastorate, and who views the small church as the first necessary stop on the way up the ecclesiastical ladder of success. This type of pastor normally enters the small church with a sudden burst of energy, and a desire to accomplish as much as possible in a short amount of time. The priority is program development, rather than people. The church people become overwhelmed by all the organization and programming but try to do what the pastor wants done.

After a stay of eighteen months to three years, the pastor with the stepping stone mentality moves on to a larger church. The laity are bitter that the pastor has moved before they really got a chance to know him/her, and just when some new programs were beginning to develop. But subconsciously they also heave a sigh of relief that things will at least get back to normal.

The third type of pastor who has frequently been called to serve in small churches is the pastor with the missionary mentality. This is the type of pastor who views the small church as a place to do his/her personal, sacrificial mission. The pastor sacrifices self in order to accept a call to a small church to help those poor people.

Such pastors normally have preconceived notions of what needs to happen in that church. And the objective of the pastor with the missionary mentality is to change the people in that small church so that they will be more normal. The pastor with the missionary mentality usually runs into conflict very quickly, and his/her entire pastorate becomes a tempestuous battle.

One underlying problem with all three types of small church pastors is that they are often cultural foreigners. This is especially true in small, rural churches. The pastor is an urban, upper middle class, seminary educated pastor, who possesses a certain cultural superiority over the laity of the small church. Therefore, the pastor feels that he/she knows what is best for that congregation. Any program development becomes the pastor's thing. In any case, the pastor is usually gone in less than five years. And in each case it is not the church laity that is the problem. It is the pastor who is the main problem.

Isolating the Variables

Having stated that the pastor is often part of the problem in small churches, it now becomes necessary for us to try to discover some of the key variables that might lead to pastoral effectiveness. As a basis we will concentrate briefly on a case study of some rural Presbyterian church pastors in West Virginia.

In the spring of 1976 I designed and carried out a survey of twenty Presbyterian pastors in West Virginia. This survey included 80 percent of the pastors in our Presbytery who were serving rural churches and had been serving in their present field for at least two years. The pastors were of various ages, backgrounds, and experiences. Four of those interviewed were not presently serving rural churches, but had completed a pastorate with a small church as recently as one year prior to the survey.

The questions were designed to gain as much information about the pastors, the churches served, and their approach to ministry as was possible. Part of the questionnaires were completed in written form and returned, while part were completed through interviews and their responses recorded.

The questions were divided into the following general categories: (1) personal background and experience, including such information as age, seminary training, the type of family background, years of experience in the pastorate, and personal theological understandings; (2) cultural understandings and attitudes toward rural life and ministry with rural churches, including values and lifestyle conflicts; (3) general background of the churches being served including type of community, size of the church field, number of years served with that church field; (4) approaches and emphases in ministry including categories of pastoral work and visitation, preaching, teaching, program implementation and community involvement; (5) a personal evaluation of pastoral effectiveness including the areas of church growth, program developments, and general feelings and attitudes toward the work accomplished.

The survey relates to pastors and to their personal evaluation of their ministerial effectiveness. Of the twenty pastors responding, ten judged themselves generally effective and ten judged themselves generally ineffective.

On the following page is a chart which records the responses of the pastors in several key categories. The survey was not all inclusive, but did indicate some general trends and tendencies.

87

PASTOR	PERSONAL BACKGROUND				CULTURAL UNDERSTANDING			CHURCH BACKGROUND			PASTORAL EMPHASES			
	C.A.	C.B.	P.T.	EX.	U.R.C.	E.R.C.	L.S.C.	N.C.S.	Y.	T.C.	P.F.	P.I.	T.	P.
1	YES	U	L	NONE	YES	YES	NO	2	10	R.I.	YES	YES	YES	YES
2	YES	R	C	15	YES	YES	NO	1	6	R	YES	YES	YES	YES
3	YES	U	C	10	YES	YES	NO	2	6	R.I.	YES	YES	YES	YES
4	YES	R	C	10	YES	YES	NO	1	4	R.I.	YES	YES	YES	YES
5	YES	U	L	NONE	YES	YES	NO	1	10	R.I.	YES	YES	YES	YES
6	YES	R	C	12	YES	YES	NO	2	12	R	YES	YES	YES	YES
7	YES	R	L	5	YES	YES	NO	1	3	R	YES	YES	YES	YES
8	YES	U	L	5	YES	YES	NO	1	6	R.I.	YES	YES	YES	YES
9	YES	R	C	25	YES	YES	NO	1	2	R	YES	YES	YES	YES
10	YES	U	L	NONE	YES	YES	NO	2	6	R	YES	YES	YES	YES
11	YES	R	C	NONE	YES	YES	NO	4	10	R/RI	YES	NO	YES	YES
12	NO	U	L	NONE	YES	NO	YES	2	2½	R.I.	NO	YES	YES	YES
13	NO	U	L	NONE	NO	NO	YES	2	4	R.I.	YES	NO	YES	YES
14	NO	U	L	8	NO	NO	YES	1	3	R.I.	NO	YES	YES	YES
15	NO	U	L	NONE	NO	NO	YES	2	3	R.I.	NO	NO	YES	YES
16	NO	U	L	NONE	NO	YES	YES	2	3	R	NO	YES	YES	YES
17	NO	U	L	NONE	NO	NO	YES	2	3	R.I.	NO	YES	YES	YES
18	NO	U	L	4	NO	NO	YES	1	8	R.I.	NO	YES	YES	YES
19	NO	R	C	NONE	YES	NO	YES	2	2	R.I.	YES	YES	YES	YES
20	YES	R	C	NONE	YES	YES	YES	2	4	R/RI	YES	NO	YES	YES

Abbreviations Used

C. A. = Community Acceptance
C. B. = Community Background
P. T. = Personal Theology
Ex. = Experience Prior to this Pastorate
U. R. C. = Understands Rural Culture
E. R. C. = Enjoys Rural Culture
L. S. C. = Lifestyle Conflict
N. C. S. = Number of Churches Served
Y. = Years with this church field
T. C. = Type of Community

P. F. = Pastoral Functions
P. I. = Program Implementation
T. = Teaching
P. = Preaching
U. = Urban
R. = Rural
R. I. = Rural Industrial
C. = Conservative
L. = Liberal

On the chart on page 88 the first ten pastors are those who evaluated themselves as generally effective, and numbers 11-20 judged themselves generally ineffective. A list of abbreviations used for recording and categorizing the responses is also included with the chart. The term community background refers to the type of community in which the respondent lived most of his life before coming to his present church field. The category of personal theology refers to whether or not the respondent considered himself conservative or liberal theologically.

In general, the survey showed the following trends. First, there seemed to be very little correlation between personal background and pastoral effectiveness. Of the ten who judged themselves effective, five were from urban background and five from rural. The results were identical in term of conservative or liberal theological background.

Of those who judged themselves generally ineffective, three were from rural backgrounds and seven were from urban backgrounds. Three judged themselves conservative theologically and seven moderately liberal to liberal.

There was generally no relationship between the seminary attended and pastoral effectiveness. However, only two of the twenty interviewed stated that their seminary training had prepared them adequately for rural church work. Both of them had attended seminary more than twenty years ago.

In terms of cultural understandings some correlations began to emerge. The ten who judged themselves effective all felt that they had an understanding and appreciation of rural life and enjoyed living in a rural area. Each felt that he had been well accepted into the community after several years, and none felt that his personal life-style was at odds with the culture.

In contrast, of the ten who judged themselves generally ineffective, six indicated that they did not have a firm understanding of rural culture, seven were not satisfied living in a rural area, and eight reported that they did not feel accepted into the community. All but one indicated that at some points their life-style was at odds with community expectations.

There were also some correlations that emerged in terms of the church field itself. Six who judged themselves generally effective served only a single church. Two of those were pastoring a church on a part-time basis, while earning part of their income from another source. The other four served two church fields. On the other hand only two of those who judged themselves generally ineffective served single church fields, while all of the others served multiple church situations. There seemed to be no correlation between whether or not the community was rural or rural/industrial.

In addition, several of those who were interviewed personally by me expressed a great deal of personal frustration regarding multiple church fields. Several indicated that duplication of programming and travel distances made it almost impossible to work effectively with two or more congregations. Several also added that the different backgrounds of the people in their congregations resulted in some difficulties. However, the principal frustration seemed to center on not being able totally to commit oneself emotionally to one church or the other.

Of the ten who judged themselves generally effective, only three had served that church field less than five years, and each was still serving that situation with no immediate plans to move. Only two of the ten who judged themselves generally ineffective had served more than three years with that church field.

Some correlations also emerged in the category of approach to ministry. Of those who judged themselves generally effective, all ten answered that they tried to balance their ministry between pastoral concerns and program. All said they spent a great deal of time the first eighteen months building relationships with people in the congregation. Six of the ten who were judged generally ineffective indicated that they did not emphasize general pastoral visitation and building personal relationships with the laity of the church.

Finally, there emerged a correlation between effectiveness and experience. Only three who judged themselves effective had no prior experience in the pastorate. Of the ten who rated themselves ineffective, only two had previous experience.

Therefore, the five variables that emerged in this survey, and also in an historical analysis of rural churches in West Virginia with regard to pastoral effectiveness, relate to the pastor's personal attitude toward the culture and life-style, the length of stay at the church, the size of the church field in terms of the number of churches served, the emphasis placed upon pastoral functions, and building relationships with the people in the church, and years of previous experience in the pastorate.

The Stages of Becoming a Small Church Pastor

Another finding emerging from this study was that there seems to be some natural developmental stages in a small church pastor's maturation toward effective pastoral leadership. There is no specific time frame for these particular stages of development, but in general the entire process seems to take from six to ten years.

First is the stage of building and solidifying relationship, and general community acceptance. This is the time during which the pastor comes to know and understand the local people, including their history, kinship

91

ties, and culture. It is likewise the period during which the local people begin to know and understand the pastor.

As part of this phase of community acceptance, the pastor begins to understand self in relationship to this community of people. The support group for the pastor gradually begins to center on this community of people. There is a growing self-awareness, and the pastor begins to understand and accept the pastoral expectations, and feels comfortable in his/her relationship with the people.

Second is the stage of fulfillment of the pastoral functions. The pastor is accepted as preacher, teacher, and counselor. When accepted by most of the people as counselor, this is a sure indication that the pastor is accepted and trusted. This is the stage during which the pastor can begin to work creatively with the people in program planning and development.

Finally, there is the stage of full community participant. Many small church pastors never arrive at this stage. This is the point at which the pastor is considered as much a part of the local community as anyone else. It normally coincides with the developmental stages in which the small church is beginning to reach out to do mission in the local community. As the congregation reaches out beyond survival toward mission, so the local pastor rediscovers his/her identity in direct relationship to that community of people.

Community Acceptance

There are numerous components that are involved in community acceptance for the church pastor. The fact is that when a small church pastor first enters a new pastorate, he/she is viewed in terms of role expectations, rather than his/her unique personhood. Therefore, as we have stated previously, the initial objective is to grow out of these role expectations, into community acceptance.

(1) The Call as a Means of Legitimation.

The first necessary step toward acceptance is community legitimation of the person for the task. Legitimation is the process of being accepted by the people as their pastor. Legitimation begins with call. The pastor needs to feel a genuine sense of call to the small church before the process of legitimation can begin.

Not only must the small church pastor feel a valid sense of call to that pastorate, the pastor needs to be able to verbalize this feeling of call as part of his/her own faith experience. It is important for the church laity to be able to know that the pastor has come to their church because of the urgent and exciting expectation that God has called him/her to this place, at this specific time in history.

People in rural churches are accustomed to pastors who come to work with their congregation, fresh from seminary, remain two or three years and move on. It is difficult to feel much assurance that any pastor would come to their congregation out of personal choice or any genuine sense of call. The sudden realization that a pastor chooses to move to their church field because he/she really wants to and feels a call to serve there, is the quickest means of legitimizing that individual as pastor.

I well remember when I first interviewed with the Beverly Church pulpit committee. I had been serving as associate pastor of Davis Memorial Church, a large congregation in Elkins. During our ministry in Elkins, my wife and I had become increasingly convinced that we wanted to return to a rural community, and I was equally convinced that I would probably spend the rest of my ministry working with small rural churches.

When interviewing with the pulpit committee, some of

93

our feelings of joy and excitement about returning to a rural church pastorate, were transmitted to the people. The whole atmosphere of the meeting changed as a feeling of acceptance seemed to permeate the group. It was an experience that has stuck with me. And the fact that my wife and I were both able to verbalize our own feelings about rural communities and churches, and the sense of call that we both felt at that time, helped to stimulate this atmosphere of acceptance.

This sense of call is not something that can be faked. It is either there, or not. And the church people will quickly pick it up either way. The point is, small church people are still very much attuned to hearing and sharing faith experiences. And the faith experience of their own pastor in being called to their church is most important.

The sense of call is part of what I would term a general need for a positive spiritual piety. This is not to imply that the small church pastor must be other worldly or a religious mystic. But it does imply the importance of some form of disciplined, devotional life. Personal devotional life is essential in maintaining the spiritual strength to work in the pastorate. And it is likewise essential if one is to be able to communicate one's on-going faith experience, to the people of the church.

Part of my own spiritual reawakening involved the development of a regular, devotional life. Until five years ago my own prayer life had been rather spasmodic. Since that time I have a regular time for scripture reading and prayer each day. As one might expect, it has done wonders to strengthen my own character, enlarge my relationships, and refocus my entire life. However, that in itself would not be enough. I have also taken the opportunity to share my own devotional experiences with others in the church, and it has been quite enriching.

As a matter of a fact, during January of 1976 when I

began a three-month vigil of fasting each Monday and setting aside the money saved for the One Great Hour of Sharing offering at Easter. I also preached a series of six sermons on the meditative style of life. In the sermons I shared some of my own experiences, and also those of some of the church fathers and medieval mystics. The response from the people in the congregation was much more positive than I had previously anticipated. Since that time I have had many other opportunities to talk about the meaning of faith and personal meditation with numerous individuals. The sharing of my own faith experience and my own personal sense of call has been an essential component of becoming accepted into the local community.

At any rate, it can be generally stated that the willingness to share one's personal feeling of call and devotional life, is important in becoming an accepted member of the local community. It is the initial means through which the level of trust is raised, and the individual pastor is validated for his pastoral responsibilities and tasks. It is a means through which the church people can begin to share their own faith experiences with one another and with the pastor. And perhaps most important, it is the means by which the local church people become assured that their pastor has chosen to be with them because of a feeling of commitment and call, and not because there is no better place to go.

(2) Personal Attitudes and Life-style.

The second thing that determines the level of community acceptance for the pastor is the whole area of personal attitudes and life-style. As we have mentioned previously, it is essential that the small church pastor, regardless of background, not be burdened with feelings of cultural superiority. What this means is that one must not only be accepting, but actually enjoy life amidst that community of people. There is nothing that will prevent community acceptance more than attempting to impose culturally foreign attitudes and values on people.

This is related to what we previously termed the "missionary mentality." The attitude of cultural superiority once typified by most denominational missionary endeavors, resulted in attempts to reculturalize whole nations of people. It eventually gave rise to cries of "Missionary Go Home."

For instance, if one comes to a rural West Virginia parish with the attitude that through personal sacrifice, he/she is going to help those poor people improve their lives, that pastor is doomed to failure from the start.

In fact, quite the opposite must be true. In rural areas, it is quite advantageous if one appreciates the normal culturally accepted leisure time activities such as gardening, hunting, fishing, mountain music, and crafts. This doesn't mean that one has to be a sportsman, or become a mountaineer to be a rural church pastor. But if one expresses a genuine appreciation and understanding for the accepted leisure time activities of rural people, it does help to establish an initial point of contact.

Work with one's hands is always valued by rural people. Gardening, carpentry, cooking, sewing, are all creative activities that help people express who they are. It is important to know and appreciate this fact.

The problem of language and communication also needs to be understood. An impressive vocabulary will not necessarily help to win acceptance by small church people. Communication by anecdote and story are usually much appreciated. Again, this doesn't imply that one has to be able to "spin a yarn" to be accepted. But it does help if one has an understanding of such basic cultural phenomena.

One of the most important elements in terms of attitudes and life-style is personal morality. Tolerance for various types of personal morality varies greatly between communities and congregations. For example, there are some small congregations that might be accepting of social drinking. There are others where this would not be accepted. Many small church laity are conservative when it comes to personal morality, and this is one battle which the small church pastor should avoid if possible.

Probably the most important personal attitude for the rural church pastor to possess is to be person oriented. The pastor must relate to the people as a person, as well as a minister.

This involves the basic nature of small churches. The small church exists to be, not to do or be done to. People want to relate to one another. They want to know their pastor. It is more important to be a person than to fulfill one's role. And this a pastor must understand.

Doing program is a priority for most pastors. This is how we have been taught to measure our own effectiveness. But in small churches, people are more important than programs and schedules. People must have the priority. Structure and scheduling is fine up to a point. But people must come first. One has to be willing to change plans, alter schedules, rework objectives, even at the last minute in order to relate to the needs of the people. The relationship with the people is the priority, not programming and accomplishments.

(3) The Length of Pastorate.

The third general area that affects community acceptance is the length of pastorate. It is important to realize that one will not be accepted as part of the community unless one is willing to make a long-term commitment to the congregation and the community.

It is a fact that throughout the history of small churches in our area, pastors have been generally ineffective by all standards of measurement, unless they have

97

been willing to stay with a single pastorate at least five years.

It is no doubt true that those pastors who have been willing to stay five years or more in a single pastorate, have been comfortable and happy enough with the situation that they have been able to work more effectively. So it is difficult to draw a direct cause and effect correlation between length of stay and pastoral effectiveness.

However, it is also true that in small churches it takes two to three years to get to know the people and become trusted. The most effective years of ministry begin after the third year. Therefore, it must be assumed that length of stay is an important consideration in terms of community acceptance.

(4) The Single Church Field.

A fourth element that affects community acceptance is whether or not one serves a single church field. It is very difficult to serve a multiple church parish and become an accepted part of any one community. The small church pastor who becomes accepted as a part of the local community lives in that community and spends most time and energy there. And most important, the pastor gives personal loyalty and emotional commitment to that group of people.

It is becoming apparent that it is easier to hold a secular job to supplement income, and serve as pastor of a single church on a part-time basis, than to serve as pastor of a multiple church field. It isn't just the division of time that creates problems. It is the division of loyalties. To become part of a small community you have to give yourself to that congregation and community. There is no way an individual can subdivide loyalties.

(5) Participating in Community Life.

It is essential if a rural church pastor is to become accepted as a part of the local community that this person must be supportive of the community. It is important to support and participate in community events and celebrations. One needs to be supportive of the local schools and other institutions. It is necessary to participate in committees and various community meetings when called upon to do so. If one is to become part of community, one must be a community participant.

Undergirding all of this is a fact that we have reiterated. The small church pastor must grow to know the people well enough that he/she no longer relates to them in terms of a social role. When the small church minister is no longer thought of only in terms of being a preacher or a pastor, but is known and thought of as a person, that pastor has become part of the local community.

(6) Making Changes.

One additional fact needs to be borne in mind when discussing this process of community acceptance of the small church pastor. This involves the whole area of making changes.

It has been the practice of many small church pastors to instigate certain changes in the church within the first few months of starting a new pastorate. Sometimes these involve changes in the order of worship. Sometimes they involve changes in the actual structure of the church boards or sessions.

In one particular instance a small church pastor proposed that the church session go to a rotation system at his second session meeting. What that immediately communicated to the session members was that the pastor didn't like them and wanted them to rotate off as soon as possible. A win/lose power struggle ensued and the pastor's relationships with certain members of that session were irreparably damaged.

As a general rule a small church pastor should not propose any major changes for at least one year. This even includes major changes in the order of worship. After the relationships of the pastor with the members of the congregation have been solidified, and a measure of trust exists, changes can slowly begin to occur.

However, in small churches, all changes should be approached slowly. These should never be arbitrarily done by the pastor. In most cases they should have the concensus of most of the members of the church. This is essential if the changes are to have the desired effect.

The Approach to Work

We have generally been dealing with the process of establishing and solidifying relationships between the small church pastor and the members of the congregation. It is next necessary to deal with the pastor's major emphases and major approach to work in the small church.

(1) Who's In Charge.

The small church pastor cannot be the "boss" of the congregation and be effective. Responsibility for decisions, and the implementation of programs must be a shared responsibility with officers and other members of the congregation. This relates to everything that the pastor does.

It needs to be emphasized that at some point the pastor needs to decide which areas of ministry will consume the most time. It is important at the outset to involve the local church people in this determination. And it is quite important on a regular basis to keep the church board or session informed of what has been happening. It's a good idea at the monthly meeting to report on visits, meetings that have been held, and how one's time has been spent. After the first six months or year, it is a good practice to have a major planning conference with the session or church board to discuss in more detail the areas of ministry that are most important to the congregation. This can be determined by informal discussion and by arriving at a general concensus. Or if it seems desirable, one might wish to work out a formal survey with the whole congregation. Once this is done, it is most important to schedule one's time so that it reflects the priorities of the congregation.

It is important to take this basic approach of involving the congregation in decision making in terms of all areas of ministry. Small churches often have a tradition of the pastor attempting to run the whole show. As a result, the congregation frequently abdicates responsibility for what happens.

The small church pastorate is one in which the congregation must determine the basic decisions. The pastor cannot become authority figure or chief manipulator, or he/she will remain in vertical relationship, apart from the people. Effective pastoral work implies that the small church pastor enable the people to make and implement their own decisions about congregational life and ministry.

Along this same line it is essential to understand that win/lose battles are totally destructive in small churches. Relationships are too important and people too few to be able to sustain win/lose battles. If the pastor sees things which must be done and there is strong resistance, he/she must work patiently and slowly and not draw battle lines. The people have to be in charge in rural churches, not the pastor.

(2) The Pastoral Functions as a Priority.

As we have previously discussed, the general pastoral functions must be a priority in small churches. And this means pastoral visitation and calling.

It is especially important in the first year or so to visit in the homes of church members. This is the best way to get to know the people personally. After good relationships are established, visiting among the church members may not have to be stressed as much.

101

However, personal visitation in times of illness and bereavement is essential. This is perhaps the central pastoral function. And prayer by the pastor at such times is expected.

It might also be added that the rituals of weddings and funerals are also very important pastoral functions. As was explained in a previous chapter, weddings and funerals are usually community events that transcend all differences. In most instances, the traditional types of services are expected. With regard to funerals, in most rural areas it is expected that the pastor be present at the funeral home for at least part of the family visitation time.

The pastor is expected to take the lead in visiting inactive and prospective members. It is a good practice to involve lay people in visiting with the pastor in the homes of inactive members. They usually know the people and have a better entree. Also, pastoral visitation of prospective members accomplishes little unless it is accompanied by lay visitation.

At any rate, the personal contact of visitation is an important part of pastoral work in the small church. A large block of any pastor's time should be spent in this endeavor.

Counseling in small churches becomes important only after being in the community for several years. The first few years there will probably be only infrequent opportunities for counseling. After three to five years in the same parish, this may become an important focus of pastoral work. Developing trust is the key ingredient in this area of pastoral ministry.

(3) Preaching and Teaching.

It is obvious that preaching and teaching constitute another important area of work for the rural church pastor.

The Sunday morning worship is central to the life of

the small church. Therefore, preaching remains a most important function that must be taken seriously. There is wide tolerance of the type of preaching. However, sermons do need to be biblically based. Topical sermons are usually not received too well.

In addition, vast experimentation in forms of worship is usually not received well in small churches. There can be some variety in forms of worship. But again, if one is to change the order or form of worship, it is best to work such changes through the session or church board.

The small church pastor is a teacher. That teaching responsibility should principally be viewed in terms of helping laity expand and develop their own belief system. The object is not to teach your own personal theology to the people.

Teaching can be done through sermons, officer training, Sunday school classes and the like. Special Bible study classes are also common in small rural churches as a means of teaching.

In fact, the midweek Bible study can become the best setting for teaching. There is no real time limit in most instances, and depending upon the format there is ample opportunity for open sharing and discussions.

Work with youth is part of the teaching responsibility, and it is considered important in most small congregations. Involving local youth in general worship and life of the congregation can do a great deal to enhance the vitality of a church. Youth choirs are normally greatly appreciated by the adult laity, as are special children's times during the worship service.

Yes, the small church pastor has an important teaching function. The teaching and preaching ministry are central to the work of small churches.

(4) Personal Stewardship.

The small church pastor needs to be involved in the local congregation through personal financial support.

Although church members might seldom openly express the importance of substantial financial support from their pastor, the expectation is usually there.

One cannot be an effective leader of a congregation, and expect sound stewardship commitment from church laity, if one is unwilling to set a certain standard for giving. This is not spoken of openly, because to most small church people, giving is a very personal thing. But the church people know who supports the church. And lack of stewardship commitment by the pastor is not conducive to effective ministry.

(5) The Prophetic Task.

The small church pastor certainly has a prophetic responsibility too. And generally speaking the prophetic task falls into two main categories.

First, it is usually the impetus of the pastor that a congregation will begin to look at human need locally. The pastor is in a unique position to stimulate interest in and commitment for the church's involvement in ministry to meet the needs of people in the community. This is essential if the church is to be the foundation for the regeneration of community life.

Secondly, the small church pastor is in a position to lift the vision of the local church people and community beyond themselves to the larger spheres of life today. It is true that one of the great difficulties with small churches is the inherent limited vision that concentrates only on the parochial concerns of the local community. This smallness of vision often prevents churches from being the church.

A local district superintendent of the United Methodist church stressed at a meeting that he did not like the term small church. "A church is only small," he said, "if its vision and view of ministry is small." It is this smallness of vision that often infects many of our rural churches. And the small church pastor constantly has the task of expanding the concerns of the people in both the church and the local community.

Training for Small Church Pastors

The pastor plays a key role in enabling a small church to move through all the developmental stages of revitalization. And the ability to serve this enabling function demands special understandings, skills, and training.

Theological seminaries have been woefully inadequate in offering the type of training needed to prepare persons for small church ministry. There is no indication that this situation will soon change.

I believe it to be primarily the responsibility of the middle church judicatory to fulfill this need to train pastors for work in small churches.

The Presbytery of Greenbrier has begun to develop a pastoral education program aimed at easing the transition of pastors into a local church. This program is proving especially beneficial to the small church pastors. There are three phases to the program.

(1) The Pastor Start-Up Program.

The Pastor Start-Up Program consists of a series of three meetings with the pastor and session led by a group facilitator. These meetings are aimed at building relationships and helping the pastor make an effective start in working with the church.

The first meeting is designed to help the pastor and session members share their histories. It greatly helps the process of team building. The second meeting is designed to have pastor and session members share their ideas on what are the most important areas of ministry for the pastor to concentrate time. The third meeting is designed to help the session members share with the pastor how their church is organized and what are its main program concerns, and have the pastor share his/her major skills and weaknesses.

105

(2) New Pastor Orientation Program.

A second component of the pastor training program of Greenbrier Presbytery is the new Pastor Orientation Program. This is a series of three three-day seminars and participation in each is required of all new pastors in the Presbytery. The first seminar includes a general introduction to the area, and to the Presbytery. It also deals with guidelines on how to start up a new pastorate effectively. The second seminar is an introduction to the culture of the region, with specific concentration on religion, and understanding how to work with small churches. The third seminar deals with developing programs.

(3) Eighteen-Month Pastor Assessment Process.

The third component being built into the pastor education program is an Eighteen-Month Pastor Assessment Process. It is a fact that in most pastorates there is usually a spiritual and emotional low point somewhere between the first and second year.

The Eighteen-Month Pastor Assessment Process is a three-day seminary aimed at helping the pastor reflect upon his/her ministry up to that point, evaluate strengths and weaknesses, and project continuing education needs and plans for the next three to five years.

All three pastor education programs have proven quite beneficial to the pastors who have participated. It is hoped that such training programs will facilitate more effective, longer, and happier pastorates.

The small church pastor plays an essential role in the revitalization process. But it is important to understand that the revitalization process must never be totally dependent upon the pastor, or it will fail. The real key to the pastor enabling revitalization is that the pastor be part of the group, part of that community of people. One must offer leadership, yes. But it is essential that the real redevelopment of the congregation reflect the ideas and work of the people, not just the pastor.

The pastor gives ideas, supports, helps, and encourages. But the pastor cannot become the director or sole initiator of change. The process of revitalization must be of, by, and for the entire congregation, or it will not last. The pastor's most essential role is to be part of that community of people, and help them to reach their potential.

CHAPTER NINE

Reaffirmation and Planning for Victory

It is now necessary to focus more detailed attention on each of the stages in the process of revitalization. What we are really speaking of initially is an attitudinal transformation from a survival mentality to new identity and vitality. In this chapter we will be dealing with the first two stages of the process of revitalization, that of reaffirmation and of planning for early victories. These are separate steps in the revitalization process, but they are very closely related and sometimes happen simultaneously.

The problem that is being dealt with in these early stages is, of course, the survival mentality. Members of small congregations have been told so many times in so many ways by people and institutions within American culture that they are weak and impotent, that many have believed it. Many laity in small churches accept the fact that their congregation is on the continuous brink of dissolution. They know that their numbers are relatively few. They are aware that finances are a continuous problem. They recognize that they have difficulty in carrying out successful programs. Therefore, the inevitable conclusion seems to be that they are indeed weak, with no unique purpose, and must concentrate all their attention on institutional survival.

This survival mentality prevents any growth, inhibits program and kills mission. Worst of all it is predicated upon false values which are reinforced by the denomination and society as a whole. Therefore, the attitudinal transformation entails in part, a reassessment of values. And this means a reaffirmation of some traditional values of the past.

The Process of Reaffirmation

The pastor is probably the key in this attitudinal transformation within the small church. And the initial approach that some small church pastors have taken is to begin by spending a great deal of time reaffirming the validity and importance of that small group of people. Through sermons, teaching, conversations with individuals, a positive attitude toward the people and the church must be manifested. And above all else, the cultural values of bigness and productivity as equaling success must be challenged.

In a sense what is needed is the establishment of a new mindset that small is important, small is good, small is essential, and small is uniquely powerful. This can certainly be supported from the standpoint of the Gospel. It wasn't twelve thousand but twelve people who began the transformation of Roman society in the first century. The early Christians did not gather by the hundreds and thousands. They often gathered by twos and threes. It was in part the deep personal concern for people that originally made the Christian Gospel so appealing. And it is the close personal relationships inherent in the small church, that make it so incredibly appealing today, in a massive and depersonalized society. So the first reaffirmation that needs to be made is the reaffirmation that small is good.

Related to this is the reaffirmation of the interpersonal

109

support system of the small church. Most small churches possess a strong interpersonal support system. This is perhaps the most important characteristic of small churches. For it is through the support system that the individual member receives his or her own emotional strength for living.

The support system of many small churches transcends the membership boundaries of the congregation and encompasses the larger community. This support system particularly becomes important in times of grief or illness.

In rural areas, when a family member dies, church and community unite to support the bereaved. Food is brought to the home. People are available to answer the phone and greet visitors coming to the home. Everyone is available to help if called upon. The same type of support exists in times of illness.

These natural support systems in small churches need to be recognized and affirmed. Building upon the fellowship ties through regular family night dinners, and other social occasions is helpful. Any program that serves to bring people together for sharing and fellowship, undergirds and strengthens the support system of the congregation.

Another important element in the stage of reaffirmation is reaffirming the history and tradition of the congregation. Many small, community based churches, have a strong sense of historical identification. This is not only true in terms of the general history of the church, but also in terms of the church's relationship to the community. Small churches have a sense of turf. The people feel a sense of belonging to a particular geographic space. The church belongs to community and vice versa. Its life and history is deeply interwoven in the fabric of community life in general.

In the process of reaffirming the history of the church

110

in relationship to the community, hidden or forgotten history can be renewed. For instance, many rural churches in West Virginia had a history of denominational cooperation long before the industrialization of the region. They frequently shared a common building, a common pastor, and did most things together. Rediscovering and reaffirming this type of history can have a very positive effect upon a congregation.

History and tradition need to be celebrated in small churches. And the church can become the center for communitywide celebrations when reaffirming history.

The town of Beverly has a community week each summer. And the local Methodist and Presbyterian churches play a major role in the community celebration. One of the highlights of the week is a community hymn sing at one of the churches, supported by the entire community. The church buildings are centers of activity all during that week.

Related to the whole matter of reaffirming history and tradition for a congregation, is the importance of the church building itself. The concept of the church building as the center of community is perhaps the most essential development in a small church rediscovering its roots.

As has been mentioned previously, in a very real sense the church building is regarded as sacred space. Rural church buildings are often located in the center of town or in a place of high visibility. The history of the church building is an essential aspect of the congregation's history. For it is the physical building that transmits the feeling of historical continuity and the sense of identity with a certain geographic space.

As an example, the Beverly Presbyterian church building is located in the center of town. It was rebuilt after the Civil War as a community effort. Much of the history of the church is symbolically represented in the building

111

itself. The education wing was constructed during a period when the congregation was experiencing growth and vitality. The rug in the church sanctuary was woven during the same time as a 4-H community project. The building is very important to the people.

What is important in terms of attitudinal identity is the concept of the building in the minds of the people. Although the members respect and are attached to the ediface, it has been the official policy of the church for many years to encourage community groups to use the building. The church has been used regularly by the 4-H, the county historical society, and various other groups. It is even used as a refreshment stand during Beverly Community Week.

The church building can clearly project to the community how the congregation envisions its place in community. It can be an important symbol of community and help to solidify relationships between church and community. And historically most small churches at one time were a center for community activity. Rediscovering and affirming this type of history is an important part of the revitalization process.

A word of caution needs to be added in relationship to the historical identity of small churches. Rural congregations can become so tied to history and tradition that it is immobilizing. Historical identification must always be tempered by the reality that the church is in the world to affect community and the world now. And this might demand newness and change. However, the change that comes will occur most effectively when done as a result of reaffirming history and tradition.

The pastor certainly plays an essential role in reaffirming the history and tradition of the congregation. The interest shown in learning the history and background of the congregation will have a positive effect upon the members.

Lending support to traditional celebrations and encouraging the history of the church to be recorded and celebrated in various ways, will build relationships with the people, as well as enable them to feel more positive about their church.

A fourth component of the process of reaffirmation involves reaffirming and undergirding the cyclical rituals of life as important community celebrations. Birth, puberty, marriage, and death are natural cycles of life, that need to have very special emphases in any congregation. It is essential to understand the traditional expectations of these cyclical rituals. These are not normally points at which the small church pastor should be innovative. Rather the task is to understand the tradition and fulfill the pastoral role as completely and effectively as is possible. If changes in these rituals are made, they should be made with the careful consultation and understanding of those involved.

In the Beverly Presbyterian Church, baptism is an important celebration, symbolic of the health and life of the congregation. My first two years as pastor of the Beverly church I had only one infant baptism. This was somewhat indicative of the state of the church as having no younger people.

In the next couple years several younger families became active in the church, and the number of infant baptisms increased dramatically. This became an important symbol to church members that the congregation was becoming active and vital. But beyond that the infant baptisms are often community type rituals, based upon kinship. In most infant baptisms, new people are present in church. Grandparents, brothers and sisters of the parents, friends of the family are all present for these community events.

There have also been several adult baptisms of young men who have become part of the church. In each case

113

the wife had already been baptized. The fact that these men took the step of openly affirming a faith commitment and becoming a part of the church, has been a major breakthrough in opening the church to the larger community around.

Marriage is another cyclical ritual in the church that is indeed a community celebration. I have had numerous weddings in the past seven years. Some have been for church members, but most were not. These community weddings demonstrate legitimation of the marriage covenant.

An illustration of contrasts will clarify my meaning. My first year as pastor of the Beverly Church, I had two weddings at Christmastime. One was the wedding of my wife's brother in Ohio, and the other was a wedding in the local community.

In the former wedding ceremony, the couple had written their own wedding service. It had been carefully thought out, and was quite a beautiful and meaningful ritual. It was a large church wedding, but throughout the ceremony I had the distinct feeling that two individuals were participating in a very personal and private ritual, in public.

In contrast to that, the wedding in Beverly was a total community event. The two being married were not members of the church. However, the church building was packed by both church members, and other people from the community. The service itself was very traditional. And yet it was very much a community celebration, not a private ritual.

The most difficult experience in a small church is death. It is another time during which the church is the center of community life. In the fall of 1975, two people who were longtime pillars of the Beverly church died two months apart. They had been residents of the community for several decades, and everyone knew and respected both of them. The funeral services of both were major occurrences in the community. There were as many Methodist and nonchurch members present, as Presbyterians. And the most difficult result was that following these two deaths the entire church and community entered a period of mourning.

The congregation had just begun to pick up some new vitality prior to this occurrence. But with those two deaths everything stopped. A pall of depression hung over the congregation for several months. I was beginning to believe that the church was on the brink of total collapse when the grief process ran its course, and the congregation began to exhibit some new life.

In addition there have been several occasions when the local Methodist pastor and I have jointly held funeral services. In each case the person who died had had close relationships with both congregations. In conclusion, the experience of death in a rural area affects the entire community, and the church is definitely the center of support and life. Grief is public, and felt by all.

The one cyclical experience of life that I have felt is not publicly affirmed the way it should be is puberty. Traditionally in the Presbyterian church when young people reach the age of twelve or thirteen a communicants' class is held, which is about six or eight weeks in duration and is a study of the meaning of church membership. At the conclusion of the study (usually on Easter Sunday) the members of the communicants' class are publicly received as adult members of the church.

The problem is that there really is no opportunity to recognize and affirm the full process of adulthood that is beginning to occur. Therefore, at Beverly we attempted a different approach with the communicants' class in 1978. We planned three weekend retreats between January and March, where several adults met with the four boys and one girl who were becoming communicant

115

members. During these three weekend retreats there was a great deal of individual attention given to each of the young people. There was not only an emphasis upon studying the meaning of church membership, but also discussions about sexual and emotional maturity. That communicants' class experience became more of a total ritual of adulthood.

In summary, the cyclical rituals of life are definitely times during which the small church increasingly is viewed as the center of community life. And they are important points for reaffirming the basic importance of the church.

Planning for Victories

As the process of reaffirmation progresses it is important that a small church begin to experience some successes. This first entails some limited new programming by the second year. And these programs must be limited in scope, and planned thoroughly to ensure success. It is also essential that these programs reflect the goals of the people of the church.

As an example, during my second year as pastor of the Beverly congregation some of the people voiced a strong concern for the Sunday school. Therefore a meeting was set up to discuss what could be done. What was eventually decided was that the first need was to enlist some substitute teachers who would be available when the regular teachers were absent. Secondly, it was decided to place a periodic emphasis upon the Sunday school in the worship service.

The two plans were carried out. They were very limited, easily attainable objectives. The interesting thing was that as a result of those two minor changes, the Sunday school really did pick up considerably. It was an important victory for the church.

Two other initial program developments were attempted that year. A weekday youth club was established, and the fall stewardship program was strengthened. Both new ventures were limited in scope, both worked well, and helped the general vitality of the church. The experience of success, of planning something and being involved in its success, did much to overcome an inherent defeatism in that congregation.

Victories are not limited to programs, however. One of the most important victories relates to the pastor. Small church people are so used to their pastors leaving by the third year, that when that milestone passes, and the pastor has no plans of leaving, the congregation experiences new vitality. This is a major victory for any small church—keeping the pastor.

The final type of victory that is needed to help the attitudinal transformation within a small church is gaining one or two new members. It doesn't take many. Just a few members adds greatly to the life of any small church. This is especially true if the new members have young children. It is perhaps the most important victory, the most important symbol of new life and hope to members of small churches. For with the addition of new members, their institutional survival becomes secured. And for the first time they are able to begin to look beyond survival toward a new identity and mission.

CHAPTER TEN
Discovering Identity

The third stage in the revitalization of the small church is discovering a new identity. One of the basic attitudinal problems with small churches that are suffering from the survival syndrome is that they have no sense of unique purpose of mission. Part of the sense of failure emerges from the fact that they compare themselves primarily with larger congregations. Therefore, they measure their own purpose and success in terms of size and growth.

The need is for small congregations to discover their own unique sense of identity, and orient the life of the congregation toward the purpose and mission. The discovery of identity by a congregation involves a careful process of study, which involves as many people from the congregation as is possible.

The Components of the Study

This discovery of identity needs to begin with a study of theology. One of the most far-reaching results of industrialization upon religious life in America was the collapse of traditional belief systems. There is no uniformity of belief today, even at the denominational level. And theological confusion at the local church level is usually much worse.

If one asks the average member of a congregation

what he/she believes, one is apt to hear a halting, unsure response. The average lay person has little opportunity to carefully think through what he/she believes. If carried over to an entire congregation the lack of clear belief is even more acute.

It is difficult to fathom any congregation discovering a new sense of identity, without first developing some basic theological presuppositions on which they agree. And the most essential element is some theological understanding of the purpose and mission of the church.

Similarly, congregations need to rediscover their denominational ties. Many small congregations have strained relations with the denominational judicatories at best. Persons in small churches need to gain a fresh understanding of what it means for them to be part of a specific denomination. They need to understand how the denominational structure works so they can participate in decision making that affects their lives.

Finally, each small church needs to study the meaning and purpose of worship, and create its own form of worship. The worship service is often the sole responsibility of the pastor. One of the first changes a new pastor normally makes is to change the order of worship to reflect his/her beliefs about worship. This is frequently done with little or no consultation from the congregation, or church board.

The worship service of a congregation should reflect the identity of that group of people. And as a small church struggles to discover its identity, it is only natural that the members of the congregation should become involved in creating a form of worship that is reflective of who they are becoming.

The Teaching Task of the Pastor

A key element in the development of this new identity in small churches is the role of the pastor as teacher. In the past the pastor has been part of the problem in this lack of identity in small churches. For instance, often the small church pastor has approached the theological task in terms of changing the theology of the people by teaching his/her own theological viewpoints.

Due to short-term pastorates by pastors of differing backgrounds, the result has been more theological confusion among the laity. The same results from pastors who precipitously change the order of worship to reflect their own ideas and needs. The teaching task of the pastor needs to be understood.

The pastor is a teacher. But that task should not be oriented toward changing the people to think more like the pastor. Rather the teaching task of the pastor is to understand the culture, history, and life situation of the people, and enable them to study together and create their own theology and worship forms. This does not mean that changes in thinking and theological growth and maturity will not occur. Such growth will be an inevitable result.

The point is that a pastor cannot force and direct this process of growth in people. This must be a natural process that occurs as people in a congregation learn how to study the Bible and theology together and reflect upon their own life situation.

Therefore, the teaching task of the pastor is to afford opportunities for reflection and growth to occur, and to help the people bring together their various beliefs into a consistent theology of life.

A Case Study of Methodology

The following is a brief case study of one way in which a local congregation can be encouraged to begin to develop a system of belief. It was a method that was used at the Beverly church, and has also successfully been used in other congregations. It is based upon involving as many members of a congregation as possible in a joint study of theology and denominational ties. The basis of this program of theological growth is small group study. It developed in this manner.

In the spring of 1977 through a congregational goal setting process, the church decided to begin a yearlong program aimed at congregational recommitment. The focus of the program was to involve the entire congregation in a study program that would eventually culminate in a commitment Sunday when all members would recommit themselves to the life and ministry of the church. The key element in the program was a six-week small group study process which would encourage members of the church to rethink their theological understandings of life.

Following the small groups studies, participants would develop a theological statement of membership commitment that would be used on commitment Sunday, which was tentatively scheduled for the Sunday following Easter in 1978. In addition, the church session would engage in a separate study which would be aimed at clarifying the specific obligations and duties of elders.

A task group of four persons volunteered to plan and implement the study course for the congregation. As pastor I was to work with the task group to help them design and teach the course.

There were to be six meetings of each study group. The meetings were designed to be an hour to an hour and a half in length, but in many instances through group concensus they were expanded to two to three hours. Each of the task force members served as a discussion leader for one of the four groups. I was a resource person and was to attend as many of the group meetings as was feasible.

There was a study outline for each group meeting, but

the focus was to be upon discussion and honest interchange of ideas and questions. The group leaders then underwent the study process themselves during October and November of 1977.

The outline of the general content of the six-week course was as follows:

The first two meetings were to focus on a general overview of the Bible. The emphasis was not upon teaching specific Biblical stories, but upon the interrelationship of the various books of the Bible as total entity.

The third meeting was a discussion of the specific constitutional questions for church membership from the Book of Church Order. The next meeting concerned general theological understandings and the need to have a belief system as opposed to separate, unrelated beliefs. The following meeting was concerned with applying theology to practical living. In these three meetings the booklet *Meet Your Church* by Joseph M. Gettys was used as a resource, although discussion was certainly not confined to the presuppositions of that book.

The final meeting focused on the actual composition by the group of a statement of what it means to be a church member. There was an initial discussion in each group on how to compose a theological statement of belief. The groups were then asked to develop an outline of key concepts that should be included in such a statement, and two persons were then chosen to formalize the statement.

The actual composition and organization of the four groups occurred in the following way: a worship service in January 1978 focused on the whole program of congregational recommitment. Following the worship service persons were given the opportunity to sign up for a group. At the congregational dinner that evening the study program was again explained and people were again given the opportunity to sign up for a group.

Each group leader was then responsible for contacting two to three inactive members of the church and attempt to involve them in his or her study group. Each group arranged its own time and location for meeting.

After all the small group meetings had been held, and each group had composed its own statement of belief, a church dinner was held in March, and the commitment statements of each of the four groups was read and discussed as a program for the evening. A representative from each of the four groups was chosen to act as a committee to combine the concerns of the four groups and compose a complete statement of congregational commitment, which was used as the theme for the worship service on commitment Sunday.

One result of the study program was an immediate increase in the level of commitment, interest, and participation on the part of a number of persons in the church. In addition, the small group study served to further develop and deepen relationships between persons in the groups. On several occasions different participants stated that this was the first time in years that they had been able honestly to discuss their questions and beliefs about religion.

It needs to be stressed that this type of theological study and development is not the first thing that can or should happen when a pastor begins to serve a small church. This process began after I had been pastor of the Beverly Church for more than four years. As was demonstrated in the previous chapter, there is a step-by-step development process that each small church must undergo before a study program such as this can be successfully implemented. This natural process cannot be rushed, or it will fail to reach fruition.

Similarly, a carefully planned process of study helped the session of the Beverly Church evolve a new order of worship. In the fall of 1977 the session of the church had a three-month study on the meaning of worship. At the same time a series of sermons on worship was preached, related to the session study.

Based upon that study the session planned a new order of worship which the church has continued to use. Again, this happened after I had been pastor of the congregation for four years.

Any small church that is involved in a process of revitalization needs to be engaged in study in order to discover new directions and new identity. As that new direction and identity emerges, the congregation is then ready to begin planning how it can achieve its mission.

Finally, this stage of rediscovering identity provides the opportunity for the small church to reassess its place in the community. Part of the study of the church must involve the purpose and mission of the church. In this way, the people in a small congregation can begin to look beyond their own church, to rediscover their mission in the local community. This is the step that enables them to envision themselves as a community based congregation.

CHAPTER ELEVEN

Planning To Do Mission

The fourth stage in the revitalization of the small church is the process of planning to do mission. This does not mean that there is no program planning in small churches prior to this stage. However, as a small church moves through the stages of reaffirmation toward discovering a new identity, there comes a point at which a more detailed process or program planning becomes a necessity. It is this process of program planning that enables the small church to begin to achieve its new identity.

It has been stated previously that a small church is not primarily oriented toward program. The small church is primarily a relational organism. There is no small church that can or would want to develop the extensive structure and programming of larger congregations.

However, at least part of the purpose of any congregation is to do the mission of Jesus Christ. And doing the mission of Jesus Christ demands that a church be more than just a relational organism. The church, any church, must always be seeking to reach beyond itself, to extend Christ's ministry and penetrate the whole community.

For the small church doing this involves some process of goal setting and program planning. This is especially true when a small church is beginning to capture a vision

125

of a new identity, and is seeking new ways in which to carry out Christ's mission. At this juncture a key element is the method of goal setting and planning.

The Experience of Failure

It has been mentioned previously that small churches frequently have a long experience of failure when it comes to processes of goal setting and program development. There is a natural built-in negativism to any strong emphasis upon structured planning. There are numerous reasons why this is true which are rooted in the history and basic nature of the small church itself. So very often planning processes which have been attempted in small congregations have been done very poorly, and without regard to the natural relational nature of the church.

First, very often program planning in the small church is the pastor's thing. The goals are the pastor's goals. The ideas are the pastor's ideas. The program structure is the pastor's program structure. The ultimate success or failure of the programs depends totally upon the pastor. Even when effective programs are planned and carried out, when they are totally dependent upon the pastor, if he/she leaves, the programs all die.

The second major problem related to goal setting and program planning in many small churches is trying to do too much. Too many programs are planned with too many committees and task forces. In small churches there just aren't enough people to carry out a lot of programming. When extensive programming is the case, the programs usually die from the sheer exhaustion of the laity involved.

The third problem is the experience of goal setting processes that are seemingly well planned, but have no results. In such cases either the goals of the church are unrealistic, or they never graduate into specific program plans. In the case of unrealistic goals, if a small congregation is in an area that is declining with very few youth around, it is unrealistic to establish youth work as a goal. On the other hand, just writing a goal statement will not make something happen. Very careful and specific program planning must follow.

Finally, the failure of goal setting and program planning in small churches often centers on the process itself. The tolerance level of small churches for long and involved planning processes is very low. Interest begins to dim after the first few weeks. In addition, the problem of language often ensures failure. Persons who are primarily relationally oriented do not respond positively to bureaucratic, organizational language.

The point is that in many small churches, self-destruct mechanisms are unconsciously built into the goal setting/planning process, and failure is ensured. And the experience of failure is the most difficult obstacle to overcome in goal setting and planning with small churches.

Principles of the Planning Process

Goal setting and planning processes need to be designed specifically with the small church in mind. In designing any goal setting process for the small church there are several basic principles to follow.

First is the principle of limited and prioritized goals. A small church should never end up with more than three goals, and these goals should be ranked in priority order and worked on one at a time. I especially like the idea of having one basic goal per year, and then developing the major portion of the church's programs around that goal. It gives a single mission focus for the congregation, and makes it possible to achieve some real victories.

The second basic principle involved in goal setting and

planning for small churches is to involve the entire congregation in the process. Whatever is attempted in a small church needs the support of the entire church. The real mission goals of a congregation must emerge from the ideas and needs of the people. Through involving the entire congregation in the process, there is a good opportunity to enlist the commitment of people through the process itself. Goals that are not truly congregational goals will have limited success at best.

Third is the general principle of the goal setting process resulting in very clear, specific objectives and program plans. These objectives and program plans should be understandable to all, and achievable. The program plans should include specific target dates, and task force members. The more specific the program plans, the better the probability that they will be achieved.

Next is the principle of training those who are to carry out the program plans. Never give laity a job without giving them the resources and training to do the job. If lay people understand the assigned responsibility, believe in it, and are trained to do it, they will almost always carry out the task effectively.

The next principle is that the actual goal setting and planning process should be as simple and brief as possible. No goal setting process in small church should take more than six to eight weeks. If it takes longer than that, interest will wane before the process ends. Language used needs to be clearly understood by all. Terms need to be defined and chosen carefully. Never assume that the people involved already understand the process. Most small church people know very little about planning processes as such.

The goal setting and planning process needs to take into account the natural relational nature of the small church. For example, in small churches that have regular fellowship dinners, it is a good idea to build the planning

128

process around these fellowship meals. Build the process into the natural relational activities of the church. Avoid meetings that are too formalized. They should be as informal as is possible, enabling the people to relate to one another, and enjoy the entire experience.

The small church pastor should be involved in the process, but not as the primary leader. The pastor should maintain the role of being one of the participants. It is therefore best to have an outside person who has been trained to lead the process. A neighboring pastor might be able to lead the process, or perhaps someone from the denominational judicatory office. Above all else, that individual needs to be able to relate to small church people.

On-going evaluation must be built into any planning process. There needs to be regular reporting at session or board meetings on process that is being made. Someone needs to be in charge of seeing that committees are meeting and carrying out their responsibilities. On-going review and evaluation is essential.

Finally is the principle of celebrating victories. If a program is planned and carried out, it needs to be recognized. The people involved in the success of the project should be given special recognition. Centering occasional worship services around celebrating such successes can do much to lift the vision and hope of members of the congregation.

The Cycle of Planning

There seems to be a natural cycle to the planning process in small churches. Many denominational judicatories are now requiring some form of self-study and goal setting during the period when a church is without a pastor. This has several benefits.

First it seems to keep the level of interest in the church

higher during the vacancy period. Secondly, it enables the church to continue doing some programming effectively. Finally, the goal setting process often enables a congregation to do a much better job in the pastor search process.

If such planning is done in a small church that needs to undergo a process of revitalization, it is natural that most of the goals and program plans that emerge will be survival oriented. They will normally relate to gaining more members, or strengthening the Sunday school. Still, such goals do serve as a help in giving a new pastor direction on what to focus his/her attention initially.

The idea of an annual planning conference retreat for the pastor and church board or session has a great deal of merit. It gives an opportunity for building relationships, while evaluating what has been happening, and planning what adjustments need to be made.

The key to the Planning Cycle in the small church, however, is the Three-Year Goal Setting and Planning Program. Every three or four years the congregation needs to repeat a detailed self-study and planning process. This is a normal cycle for pastors in reexamining their work, and it is a normal planning cycle for any church. In a small church if three or four goals are established and prioritized, then a three-year period is the normal point at which to evaluate success and develop new goals. As a general rule this goal setting process should be preceded by a six- to eight-week mission study by the congregation as a preparation for the goal setting/planning process.

One Planning Process—The Greenbrier Model

The Presbytery of Greenbrier has established a Congregational Goal Setting Process that is used with each church when its pulpit becomes vacant. The planning process is then repeated after a new pastor has served with the congregation for three years.

This Goal Setting/Planning model is led in the local congregation by a Presbytery consultant who has been trained to use the process. The entire goal setting program takes five or six weeks.

There is an initial meeting with the church session, at which time the planning process is outlined, and the support of the session is enlisted. The session chooses a steering committee of four to six persons before the end of the meeting. At least one of those persons is from the session.

Within one week the steering committee meets with the consultant and is trained to lead the process. Detailed plans for the congregational goal setting meeting are made.

Two weeks later a Congregational Goal Setting Meeting is held, usually in conjunction with a church dinner. The purpose of the meeting has been discussed at the previous two worship services, and at other group meetings. Inactive members of the congregation have been contacted and urged to participate.

The Congregational Goal Setting Dinner is designed around small group discussions aimed at eliciting the ideas of everyone in the group on the needs of the church. The steering committee members serve as group leaders. The consultant coordinates the entire meeting. The ideas that emerge from each small group are then shared with the entire group at the end of the session.

The steering committee meets with the consultant within the next few days. Based upon data gathered at the Congregational Goal Setting Meeting, goal statements are written. At the next worship service the goal statements are prioritized, and the session either adopts or modifies the goals. Within a day or two the steering committee meets again with the consultant and writes objectives and program plans for the prioritized goals. The following worship service centers on the goals and program plans that have been established, and members of the congregation are given an opportunity to sign up to work on a specific program.

The entire process is a relatively simple one and can be completed in five weeks. It requires a considerable expenditure of time and energy by the steering committee members, but is not overly involved for the rest of the congregation.

The results of the process have been quite encouraging in a number of small churches. It has served to raise the level of interest and commitment in most of the churches which have gone through the process. The average pulpit vacancy period has been cut in half, and many congregations have begun some exciting new ventures in ministry.

There are many similar types of planning processes that can be used with small churches. The real keys are to make the process understandable, simple, and achieve some quick results. And above all else, there must be a limited number of goals that are established and attempted.

The stage of learning to plan and carry out programs effectively is essential to the revitalization of small churches. Without the ability to do at least some planning and program development, there is little chance that a small church can break out of its survival mentality, and move toward becoming a community based congregation.

CHAPTER TWELVE

The Denominational Bureaucracy and the Small Church

Stating the Problem

One essential factor involved in a small church moving through these first four stages in the revitalization process is the role of the denominational middle judicatory. Unfortunately, many small churches are alienated from the denominational judicatory. The primary reason is, of course, that the middle judicatory of any denomination is totally different in nature and form from the small church. As a result, in the past these church courts have often contributed to the decline of the small church.

This state of alienation arises from three principal factors. The first is the problem of political power versus authority. People in small churches by and large are convinced that decisions and actions by church courts should be based solely upon the authority of Scripture. The Bible speaks either implicitly or explicitly to all the problems faced by the church. Therefore, the authority of Scripture should be the foundation of all decisions made by denominational judicatories.

For the past century, the higher judicatories of the major denominations have been increasingly influenced by the concept of power politics. In the past two decades as denominations have become embroiled in controversial issues such as race, war, poverty and women's rights, this emphasis upon political power has increased. Denominational judicatory meetings have frequently been epitomized divisions along conservative/liberal lines, with power block voting on controversial issues.

As a result, the emphasis has frequently been on "winning the vote" rather than working together to discern the will of God for the church at a given time in history. This type of power politics in church judicatory meetings has been difficult for numerous laity in small churches to fathom. It seems to deny the presence of the spirit of God, and this has reinforced preconceived judgments that many denominational leaders are not really servants of the Lord.

Therefore, the modern phenomenon of power politics has been a major cause of small churches becoming alienated from the higher denominational judicatories.

The second major source of alienation has been the bureaucratization of the church courts. Modern bureaucracy attached itself quite naturally to systems of church government. This has increasingly been the case in the past seventy-five years.

For instance, the Presbyterian church judicatories have been infected with an organizational mania that began in the early 1900s with a plethora of committees that quickly became self-perpetuating. By the 1950s the hiring of church executives to manage the organizational affairs of Presbyteries, Synods, and the General Assembly became quite common. By the late 1960s and early 1970s most higher church judicatories had gone through a process of total reorganization and aimed at reforming, retooling, and redirecting the organizational structures of the church. Management by objective became the craze.

The church judicatories, therefore, have been reformed as business organizations over the past one hundred years. Today they infrequently function as courts, and increasingly have invented new objectives and functions to ensure their continuity.

But the worst result has been the depersonalization of bureaucracy. It has become very difficult for local church laity to understand, participate in, and influence the decisions of denominational judicatories. Presbyteries have become the union of, by and for the clergy. For the clergy are able to understand and manipulate the processes of this bureaucratic structure.

As a result, the only real contact that the local small church has had with Presbytery has been when the Presbytery has exercised power over the congregation. This same general situation has prevailed in most of the major Protestant denominations. Bureaucratization, then, has become a major source of alienation.

The third principal reason for the increased alienation of the small church from the denominational judicatories has been a growing value conflict. Most major denominations for several decades were infected with a growth syndrome. Churches had to be a certain size (two hundred or more members) to be considered viable. The policy of many denominations was to merge or close the small congregations.

In addition, Protestantism places a strong emphasis upon doing. It was quite natural that the major denominations have always been directed toward programming for ministry. Programming means doing something for the glory of God. The problem has been that this inherent stress upon doing likewise implies that it is not valid for a small congregation to exist for the primary purpose of undergirding human relationships.

This has led to a sense of frustration, fear, and doubt in local congregations, that eventually produced defeatism. Local laity often feel that they have to ra-

135

tionalize their existence to the denominational bureaucracy. And this is normally impossible to do in terms of growth or program.

In spite of the state of alienation, it needs to be emphasized that strong denominational relations are essential if small churches are to be revitalized.

For one thing, most small churches have their identity inseparably interwoven with the denomination. Being Methodist or Lutheran is an important part of the heritage, something they could not and would not want to deny.

Secondly, the small church is dependent upon the denomination for approval and assistance if certain important changes are to occur. For instance, before a small church could share a pastor with a church of another denomination, there would have to be approval from both participating denominations. If a small church would ever reach the point of desiring a merger with another congregation, that could only occur with the approval of the denomination. Many factors that affect the future life and health of the small church depend upon the denomination.

Closely related to that is the fact that the small church is almost totally dependent upon the denomination for its pastoral leadership. The denomination exercises indirect control over the seminaries where the clergy are trained. The judicatory must approve any pastor called to a local church. And beyond that the judicatory is usually in the role of recruiting ministers for small churches.

Finally, the denominational judicatory can be an important resource for a small church. The judicatory often shares the financial load for paying the small church pastor. In addition they help in the training of local church laity, and help churches in planning for local mission.

Therefore, the small church is inseparably linked with

136

the denomination. It cannot become fully strengthened and revitalized by attempting to exist apart from the denomination. The answer then lies in strengthening, not weakening denominational ties. And the primary impetus for this must come from the denominational judicatories.

The Middle Judicatory as a Support Link for Small Churches

In the process of revitalization for small churches, denominational ties must be strengthened. And it is the role of the middle judicatory of the denomination to develop creative approaches to help overcome the bureaucratic alienation which has hindered the small church for decades.

The greatest problem that contributes to a sense of mistrust and alienation by small churches of the denominational judicatory centers on the basic philosophy of what a church judicatory is. Most denominations have traditionally stressed the importance of middle judicatory as a church court. And the concept of court carries the idea of a group of persons sitting in judgment on the local congregation.

It is true that constitutionally the middle judicatory does have certain court functions in relationship to the local congregations that must be fulfilled. But the source of resentment does not necessarily result from the specific court functions that are performed. The resentment among small church laity results when these are the only functions that are emphasized, and the judicatory is viewed as an impersonal mechanized structure that threatens the very existence of the local congregation.

People in small churches are person-oriented and they have to be related to as people. If denominational

137

judicatories are to cease being part of the problem of the small church, then people involved with the judiciary are going to have to take the time to relate to people from small churches in a personal way.

What this entails is a basic change in philosophy concerning the nature and purpose of the middle judicatory. They can no longer be centers of ecclesiastical power, undergirded and enforced by bureaucratic edict, and oriented totally toward production values of size and program development. Emphasis needs to shift to the personal caring, pastoral functions. The denominational judicatory needs to be viewed as a support link of individual congregations. This should become its primary function.

There are some basic principles that need to be assumed on the middle judicatory level to enable it to function effectively in the pastoral oversight of congregations. These certainly are not new ideas, but they are concepts that need to be implemented instead of just discussed as ideals.

The first relates to the problem of ecclesiastical power versus authority. If middle judicatories are to lose the image of manipulating the use of political power to the detriment of the individual congregations, then more participation of laity in judicatory decisions must somehow be ensured. The concept of "grass roots" participation in institutions has been so overused as to become trite. And yet, this is the first essential of an effective middle judicatory. The people, the laity of the participating congregations must feel that they are in the primary position of authority. Whether the clergy will ever trust the laity enough to invest them with the authority to decide, remains a question. The temptation for clergy to manipulate and coerce decisions on a judicatory level remains immense. But it is this very manipulation of the decision making processes that creates mistrust among the laity.

A major source of the problem is the manipulation of information, and communication. There has to be open communication and sharing of information on the judicatory level before the laity can become full participants. This entails the sharing of full information on issues and decisions that are to be made.

But it also entails the type of language used. The extensive use of ecclesiastical jargon at meetings which obscures and confuses issues serves as a means of practical disenfranchisement of the laity. This is especially true of the laity from small congregations. Ecclesiastical jargon on the judicatory level more often serves to obscure information than to share it.

The second principle that must be assumed on the denominational judicatory level to enable it to function effectively in the oversight of its congregations is the personalization of the bureaucracy. Personalizing the bureaucracy implies initially that the middle judicatory must begin to be viewed as people rather than an organizational structure. There needs to be constant personal contact between the judicatory and the local congregations by persons who are known and trusted. Judicatory meetings themselves need to become more personalized with times for sharing, fellowship, and worship. The communication of what is happening on a judicatory level needs to be shared with the local church laity regularly, and in language that is understandable.

The personalization of the bureaucracy also relates to the organizational structure itself. A denominational judicatory must frame an organizational structure of some form in order to carry out its functions. But the structure does not have to separate it from its constituent members. The structure needs to be flexible enough to change and be adapted to individual needs and situations. In other words, the principle of form following functions should be basic.

For instance, in the Presbyterian system we have too long allowed parliamentary rules and formalized regulations to govern the Presbytery, rather than allowing the needs of the churches to influence and reshape the rules. This must change if bureaucracy is to be personalized.

Finally, the church judicatory must place a higher priority on the caring, pastoral functions, than on the court functions. Time needs to be taken at meetings to talk about the good things happening in some of the churches. Representatives need constantly to be available to visit churches and help when the need arises. The middle judicatory needs to view its primary task as supporting the life of its churches. Only then will the denominational judicatory begin to be viewed as people, rather than an "it."

The third principle that will enable the denominational judicatory to function effectively in the care and oversight of their small churches is resourcing above the subsistence level. For years denominations have given just enough financial assistance, just enough help in securing pastors, just enough resources and direction to keep most of the small churches afloat. We have too long lived by the principle of supporting small churches at the lowest possible level that is feasible in order to maintain institutional survival. This must change if the small churches are to be revitalized.

The middle judicatory needs to become a primary resource for the small church. These resourcing functions fall into several categories.

First is the securing of pastors for small churches. Small churches are usually very dependent upon the denomination in securing pastoral leadership. Oftentimes the small church will remain vacant for one to three years. This is one of the most difficult problems to be overcome. Denominational judicatories need to devise systems that will enable small churches to call pastors more quickly. And stress needs to be placed on getting good, well-trained pastoral leadership.

At the same time it is at the middle judicatory level that the impetus will have to come for developing various plans for pastoral leadership for individual congregations. As a general principle, the multiple church field should be undertaken as a last resort. Shared time pastorates, tentmaking, and nondenominational community pastorates offer viable alternatives.

Secondly, the denominations have the responsibility for financially resourcing small churches for both pastoral leadership and program development and financing needs to be done at a maximum level, rather than a minimum level so that the congregation will have the opportunity to develop more effective ministry, rather than just maintain the status quo.

The financial resourcing of small rural churches at an adequate level is costly. It will entail an initial reordering of financial priorities. Also, the denomination cannot be viewed as a source of unlimited finances. Therefore, there will have to be some careful evaluation as to which churches will receive financial assistance. But the principle of providing more than subsistence funding needs to be understood and implemented.

Next, middle judicatories have an important function in developing practical systems of continuing education for small church pastors. At this point most seminaries have not developed the type of education that equips pastors to minister in small churches. Therefore, it is probable that denominational judicatories will have to develop special training programs for small church pastors. This is essential if we are to move beyond our present system of education by trial and error in the pastorate.

141

Fourthly, the middle judicatory has the essential function of assisting in leadership development for laity. One of the key problems in most small churches is leadership development. Individual small churches do not have the resources to have extensive programs in this area. Therefore it is important for judicatories to develop programs aimed specifically at small church laity. The common practice of expecting small congregations to adapt program aimed primarily at large urban congregations is self-defeating and totally impractical.

Related to leadership development is the resourcing function of assisting in program development. Many small churches are ill-equipped to plan and implement programs essential to their revitalization. The denomination judicatory can and should offer help in program planning and evaluation for small churches.

Next, the middle judicatory can be a resource in the care of pastors and churches. Denominations need to devise practical systems of pastoral care for small church pastors, and ongoing contact and care of congregations.

Finally, the middle judicatory has the responsibility of advocacy on behalf of the small church with the higher courts. The impetus for change in the denomination's constitution, and changes in structure, will have to come from the middle judicatory. In essence, the middle judicatory is the key in developing a denomination-wide strategy for the revitalization of the small church.

Case Study: The Presbytery of Greenbrier

When restructuring of Presbyteries across the General Assembly occurred, the Presbyterian Church U.S. in West Virginia faced a difficult set of circumstances. First, a large portion of the state (excluding the southern tip and the Eastern Panhandle) was to be included as one

142

Presbytery. This region had formerly encompassed three different Presbyteries. Local church members were mistrustful of being linked together in a large Presbytery with the center of power in the Charleston/Huntington area. Therefore, at the outset there was strong resistance to the restructure of trust.

Secondly, the larger Presbytery introduced an extensive geographic problem. The proposed Presbytery encompassed a large geographic area that was extremely mountainous. New roads were being built, but travel was still difficult. The population center of the Presbytery was Charleston, which meant that people from the periphery of the Presbytery would have to drive as much as 4½ hours to meetings in Charleston. That time has since been reduced to about 3½ hours with the construction of a new interstate. From the practical aspect of paying for travel, it was obvious that most meetings would have to be held in the Charleston area.

There was then the problem of resourcing. With the restructuring of the General Assembly, the funding of small churches was not the responsibility of the Presbytery. The amount of money that General Assembly and Synod was to receive remained about the same. At the same time, Presbytery would no longer receive National Ministries' support for aid to churches. Presbyteries with large numbers of small aid-receiving churches, and limited resources immediately had a resourcing problem.

Finally, the nature and size of the churches within the new Greenbrier Presbytery presented additional difficulties. Of the 118 churches in the Presbytery, 97 were below the 250-member small church guideline of the General Assembly, and 85 were below 150 members, which was our Presbytery's accepted standard for small churches. That meant that we were a Presbytery of small churches with limited resources and that the primary mission goal of our Presbytery would have to be directed toward revitalizing the small church. To compound the problem, most of the small churches were located in rural areas, and many were in former coal and lumber towns. This presented another unique set of circumstances that would have to be faced.

(1) Presuppositions in the Restructuring of the Presbytery.

The Mission and Implementation Committee that was lodged with the responsibility of creating a structure for the new Presbytery began its work with several presuppositions.

First, a continuing priority for the Presbytery for at least the first decade would have to be the revitalization of the small church. The small churches of the Presbytery had been in a general state of decline for more than two decades. That trend would have to cease if the Presbytery was to be viable. One objective was to design a Presbytery that would encourage and stimulate growth in the small churches. By that, it was not meant that all the small churches were expected to grow to the point where they were no longer small congregations. The expectation was that many of the small churches would experience some moderate growth toward an optimum level of about 100-150 members. But even more important than the growth factor was to design a strategy that would reverse the attitude of defeatism among the small membership churches and help them to believe in themselves and their unique mission in rural West Virginia.

The second presupposition was that because of the size and nature of the Presbytery there would have to be area divisions where program implementation of the Presbytery level would be carried out. The areas also needed to become the principal source of contact with the local congregations, to facilitate open communication.

Thirdly, and closely related to the second, was the problem of trust among the churches. Presbytery would have to implement and maintain a system of personal communication with individual churches. The programs of Presbytery would have to be practical and aimed at helping local congregations. Until the local churches began to believe that Presbytery could operate in a pastoral and caring way, the Presbytery would not be viable.

Next, there was a presupposition that instead of having a large full-time staff, Presbytery would eventually employ a group of Special Presbyters who would serve as pastors of small churches on a part-time basis and also carry out certain Presbytery responsibilities part time.

It was also assumed that there had to be a built-in evaluation system in the new Presbytery. The local church laity had to be involved in the evaluation and priority setting, so that they could feel a sense of ownership. Unless this could happen, no structure would be workable. Therefore, the structure that was developed had to be flexible enough to meet the changing needs of the congregation.

Finally, there was the underlying assumption that a principal function of the new Presbytery would be to secure pastoral leadership for small congregations. Between thirty and forty of the small churches of the Presbytery listed pastoral vacancies at the time of restructuring. It was assumed that a varied approach would have to be taken in order to fill these pastoral vacancies.

(2) The Structure of the New Presbytery.

The proposed structure that officially emerged from the work of the Committee on Mission and Implementation was an attempt to form a practical framework through which the Presbytery could carry out its basic functions. It was realized from the outset that the structure might have some basic flaws, but it was also presupposed that the structure was changeable at any time. It was new and somewhat different and would require some time before it could be truly functional. The following is a compilation of some of the unique features of the Presbytery structure that relate specifically to revitalizing small churches.

The purpose of the Presbytery as stated in the manual is "to care for our congregations and ministers providing pastoral support and encouragement; to interpret to the churches what we believe to be the will of God for the Presbytery and for our constituency; and to provide a means for implementing our response to the summons of our Lord to faith and obedience."

To accomplish these three purposes the Presbytery is structured with three divisions: the Division of Pastoral Care, the Division of Interpretation of God's Will, and the Division of Implementation. The Division of Pastoral Care has under its purview all of the principal caring functions of Presbytery for the congregations and pastors. The Division of Interpretation is charged with the responsibility of setting up and implementing the system of evaluation and goal setting, and the Division of Implementation is responsible to see that the goals are carried out. In addition, the Presbytery Commission on the Minister is a separate group that is responsible for most of the court functions relating to pastors and churches. The entire structure is coordinated through a coordinating council.

The Presbytery structure also provides for an area division. The Presbytery is divided into six geographic areas. Each area has an area council that meets at least

146

quarterly. The basic functions carried out through the areas are as follows:

> Development of a sense of community and support among the churches through congregational inspiration and interaction, personal and group motivation, special services and related activities.
> Carrying out the mission goals of the Presbytery especially as they relate to the life of the churches within the particular Area.
> Co-ordination of planning goal setting for local Area needs, including planning, strategy, evaluating and review . . .
> Carrying out of program functions within the Area . . .
> Submitting to the Nominations Committee the names of persons to be considered for election by Presbytery Divisions, the Nominations Committee, and as Commissioners to Synod.
> Provide a means of communication between churches and Presbytery.

The manual of Presbytery also provides for the hiring of Special Presbyters as part-time staff persons. Their work is directed and coordinated by the Presbytery Executive who is the only full-time staff person provided for outside of office personnel. The Special Presbyters, as previously mentioned, provide a means of fulfilling certain Presbytery staff needs, while at the same time providing pastoral leadership for small churches.

The final unique feature of the Presbytery structure is the process of review, evaluation and priority setting. Each year the Presbytery holds a conference meeting for the purpose of evaluation and goal setting. Prior to the meeting data is gathered from local churches throughout Presbytery relating to the needs in Presbytery programming. At the two-day meeting of Presbytery, this data is used as a basis for evaluating the work of Presbytery and setting new priorities as needed.

(3) Policies and Programs that have affected the Small Church.

For the first year and a half after restructuring in

1974, the Presbytery of Greenbrier did not function effectively. Presbytery committees and personnel were becoming oriented to the new system and there was an abundance of talk, but little practical programming. Since that time, Presbytery has begun to implement some programs that have been of genuine benefit to small churches, and hold some promise for the future.

The first major attempt by the Presbytery of Greenbrier at revitalization of its small churches was aimed at publicly affirming the importance and vitality of these congregations. In the fall and winter of 1975-76 a special task force of Presbytery developed a model for Small Church Celebrations which were to be implemented on an area basis. The purpose of the celebrations was to bring together laity from the small churches in an area for fellowship, sharing, worship, and reaffirmation.

A Presbytery-wide Small Church Celebration was held in the fall of 1975 over a three-day period. The program was then redesigned, narrowed in focus and length to a one-day event, and modeled for use by areas.

A second means of affirming the importance and nature of the small churches has been to feature a fifteen-minute presentation by a small church on its unique and vital ministry at Presbytery meetings. This has been regarded as a highlight of the meeting each time it has been done.

A second development in moving Presbytery toward becoming a support link for small churches was the emergence of an official policy for small churches. The policy gradually evolved over a three-year period, and culminated in the adoption of a *Position Paper of Small Churches* by the Division of Pastoral Care in December of 1977.

The Position Paper (Appendix A following this chapter) states the official philosophy and policies of the Subcommittee on Small Church Development of the

Division. It also outlines some of the specific programs of the Division for care and oversight of small churches. The programs of pastoral training and goal setting have been discussed in some detail in previous chapters. There are several other programs aimed at strengthening the small church that need to be highlighted.

(1) The Area Shepherd Program—The Area Shepherd Program is aimed at maintaining on-going contact and communication with every church in Presbytery. The Area Shepherd for each area is a pastor who has served a church in that area for at least three years and is known by the clergy and laity of the area. Each Area Shepherd makes a monthly phone contact with each pastor and church in the area, and at least an annual visit to each congregation. The Area Shepherds keep churches and pastors informed about what is going on in Presbytery, and also pass on communications and concerns from the churches to Presbytery office. The program has served as an early warning system for churches with problems, and has helped to raise the level of trust between small churches and Presbytery. It has become an essential means of personalizing the bureaucracy.

(2) The Policy on Chapels—One of the major breakthroughs has been the development of a policy on chapels. Chapels have never had any official status in the Presbyterian Church U.S. As a matter of fact, they are not even mentioned in the Book of Church Order, the constitution of the denomination.

The formation of chapels was a strategy for new church development that originated in Appalachia in the industrial town era. A large Presbyterian church would begin preaching services in a new town. Usually a church building was constructed. These chapels, as they were called, were directly under the oversight of the larger congregation. The rationale was that as soon as the chapel became strong enough, it would officially become organized as a congregation.

The problem was that in many cases the chapels never did become congregations, and over the years the sponsoring church often lost interest in its chapels. Therefore, these chapels continue to exist as small, independent churches, Presbyterian in name only. To compound the problem, in the 1950s and 1960s Presbyteries sometimes arbitrarily proclaimed that certain small, struggling congregations should be chapels, and placed them under the care of larger congregations. Therefore, throughout Appalachia there are numerous Presbyterian Chapels, existing as independent congregations, not officially recognized by the denomination, and often ignored by the larger sponsoring church which theoretically is responsible for oversight of the chapel.

The Division of Pastoral Care has therefore developed an official policy on chapels, recognizing their existence, and accepting responsibility for encouraging them to become organized as Presbyterian congregations. In 1978 and 1979 four chapels were officially organized as congregations by Presbytery.

(3) The Vacant Church Process—The Division of Pastoral Care and the Commission on the Minister have worked closely together to develop an effective means of helping small churches secure capable pastors. This has resulted in a Vacant Church Process.

The Vacant Church Process is predicated upon Presbytery working closely with each congregation during the entire period of pastoral vacancy. The Sunday after a pastor leaves a church field, a representative of Presbytery preaches at the church and explains the Vacant Church Process. That representative meets with the session of the congregation to go over the entire process in detail, and spends time carefully explaining the Goal Setting/Planning Process required of vacant churches. The consultant who will lead the Planning Process is also present for that meeting. Theoretically, a moderator for the session and laison with the Commission on the Minister have also been appointed by this point.

The consultant then works through the Planning Process with the congregation, culminating in a set of goals and program plans, and also a description of pastoral expectation based upon the newly adopted goals of the church. The Pulpit Nominating Committee is then trained by a Presbytery representative on how to assess dossiers, how to interview, and how to develop questions for references. During the entire vacancy period the commission laison maintains on going contact with the pulpit committee.

Through this Vacant Church Process the average pulpit vacancy period has been reduced from eighteen months to about nine months. In addition, the persons being called to small churches seem to be much more capable of working with small congregations.

(4) The Program of Peer/Colleague Support Groups— The program of Area Peer Groups was developed to give pastors much needed emotional and spiritual support from colleagues. Each peer group meets monthly, and the participants share common concerns and ideas. The meetings are structured to last about four hours. There is a special presbyter who serves as group facilitator for each of the groups.

The peer groups offer great potential for giving small church pastors who live in isolated areas, the type of support that they have needed for many years.

(5) Resourcing Christian Education—Another component of Greenbrier Presbytery's program for resourcing and supporting the small church is in the area of Christian Education. The Presbytery has a Director of Christian Education whose job is to serve as a resource person

151

for small churches. The DCE is available to work with any small church, at no cost to the local congregation.

The DCE has met with sessions and local church committees to plan overall strategies in church education. She holds workshops and training sessions for Sunday school teachers, Bible study leaders, and others who are involved in teaching. She has helped congregations in planning youth ministry. She has been available to lead special programs such as banner making and planning learning centers. Having a Christian educator who is primarily responsible for resourcing small churches has proven to be a great benefit to many small churches.

(6) Officer Training—The Presbytery Special Presbyter for Leadership Development has responsibility for developing programs of officer training for local church officers. Each fall area worships are held to train church officers in policy and theology. The training program is on a three-year cycle, and those local church officers who participate in all three workshops receive a certificate of recognition. The response to this program of elder training has been very positive in the small churches.

(7) Other Resourcing—The Presbytery of Greenbrier also offers other resource training on an area basis. Stewardship workshops are held each fall. A workshop on Reactivating Inactive Members proved to be one of the most popular workshops with the small church laity. The principle involved in all of the workshops is to hold them in areas, close to the local church, and try to involve as many small church laity as is possible.

(8) Special Presbyters—Undergirding the entire structure and program of support for small churches is the Presbytery staffing model. Except for the Presbytery Executive and DCE, each Presbytery staff person serves part time as pastor of a small church, and part time as a Special Presbyter for the Presbytery. This has

given an opportunity for a number of smaller churches to have some outstanding pastoral leadership. In addition, it has given the Presbytery staff the practical grounding to develop and implement programs of real benefit to the small churches.

Obviously the structure and resource programming of Greenbrier Presbytery is far from perfect. Some of the programs have not really developed as they should have. There is still some mistrust of Presbytery by people in some of the small churches.

Still, Greenbrier Presbytery does provide an example of one denominational judicatory that is attempting to personalize the bureaucracy and to relate in an effective way to its small churches. The point is that unless middle judicatories are willing to develop more creative ways of relating to and resourcing small churches, the revitalization of such churches becomes extremely difficult, if not impossible.

Appendix A

SUBCOMMITTEE ON SMALL CHURCH DEVELOPMENT
DIVISION OF PASTORAL CARE
PRESBYTERY OF GREENBRIER

PROPOSED POSITION PAPER

I. MISSION STATEMENT AND BASIC PHILOSOPHY

The purpose of the Subcommittee on Small Church Development of the Division of Pastoral Care is to exercise oversight and care of all the small churches of Presbytery and to develop policies and programs that will help to develop and enhance the ministry of those congregations.

Our actions in working with the small churches of the Presbytery of Greenbrier will be guided by the philosophy that the small church is a wholly different type of congregation from larger churches. It is not a small version of a large church, and therefore cannot be fairly evaluated by the same means or criteria as larger congregations.

A primary ministry fulfilled by the smaller churches in rural areas is that they serve to undergird and support community life, not just through program functions, but by their very existence. The small church exists to enable and support the fulfillment of human relationships, and not just to do program. This fact must be considered when assessing the necessary and vital nature of our smaller congregations.

While recognizing the unique nature of the small church, this cannot be used as an excuse to overlook the primary mission of the church, which is to extend the Gospel of Jesus Christ to all people. As the committee of Presbytery responsible to the small church, we cannot ignore vital areas of program development that need to occur within each local congregation.

We believe that the Presbytery of Greenbrier has a major responsibility to encourage and strengthen the development of mission and ministry within its small churches. As a committee we exist not to

155

judge the small churches, but to serve their needs and help each church develop into a more vital congregation. Facilitating this process will be the principal function of the Subcommittee on Small Church Development.

II. DEFINITIONS

1. A Small Church is
   a. A congregation of not more than 150 members.
   b. A congregation that often emphasizes human relationships over program development.
   c. A congregation in which the potential for program development is sometimes limited because of its size.
2. A Shared Ministry Church is any congregation or group of congregations which share the time and/or expense of its pastor, or receive funding from Presbytery.
3. *A Special Presbyter* is a pastor who is called jointly by Presbytery and a small church and who serves not only as pastor of that church, but also as an associate member of Presbytery staff.
4. *Shared Ministry Pastor* is any pastor who serves a shared ministry congregation.

III. RESPONSIBILITIES OF THE SUBCOMMITTEE ON SMALL CHURCH DEVELOPMENT

1. To develop and coordinate the Area Shepherd program of Presbytery for the care and oversight of all the small congregations and their pastors.
2. To evaluate and recommend to the Division of Pastoral Care programs and policies for the care and development of all the small churches in the Presbytery.
3. To oversee the annual evaluation of shared ministry churches and to make recommendations for funding.

IV. POLICIES OF THE SUBCOMMITTEE ON SMALL CHURCH DEVELOPMENT

1. *The Policy of Shared Ministry*

Any congregation which shares the time and/or expenses of its pastor, or receives funding from Presbytery is a shared ministry church. The term shared ministry refers to the reality that the financial responsibilities for paying the pastor, and the subsequent work time of the pastor are to be shared proportionally. Ordinarily, for each $3,000 provided by the Presbytery of Greenbrier toward pastoral support, the Presbytery will expect one day per week of work from that pastor, carried out under the director of Presbytery. There are several categories of shared ministry calls:

A. The Multiple Church Field—A pastor is called by and serves as pastor of more than one congregation. The time and expenses are shared between those congregations, and/or Presbytery.

B. Tent Making—A pastor is called to a church on a shared time basis for a proportion of the minimum salary established by Presbytery. The pastor also works in some form of secular employment to supplement his/her income.

C. Inter-denominational Call—Pastoral leadership and expenses are shared between two more churches of different denominations.

D. Special Presbyter—Presbytery jointly calls a pastor with a congregation. The pastor serves the church and also functions as a member of Presbytery staff.

E. Pastor to the Community—Presbytery shares the expenses of a local church pastor. Because of unique opportunities for witness and ministry, the pastor's entire work time is spent with the local church and community.

F. Student Interns—Presbytery shares the expenses of a student intern with a local congregation, or hires a student intern for a special ministry.

2. *The Policy for Oversight of Non-Shared Ministry Churches*

There are some small churches which may not meet the criteria for funding for pastoral leadership, and will therefore be unable to be served by a fully ordained pastor. The Subcommittee on Small Church Development affirms the following with regard to these small churches.

A. We affirm the importance of these congregations and are pledged to undergird their continuance and ministry, as far as the way be clear.

B. So far as is possible our committee, in consultation with the Area Shepherds, will attempt to develop some means of regular supply preaching and regular observance of the Sacraments for all such churches.

C. Through the Area Shepherd Program we are committed to maintain ongoing contact with all the small churches.

D. We will make available all other resources to these churches which might assist in the development of their ministry.

157

3. *The Policy for Oversight of Self-Supporting Small Churches*

We affirm the importance and vital nature of our self-supporting small churches and we pledge to support them and undergird their ministry in the following ways:

A. Through the Area Shepherd Program we are committed to maintain ongoing contact with all self-supporting small churches.

B. Upon request our subcommittee will assist any small church carry out a comprehensive planning process.

C. We are pledged to resourcing all of our small churches through whatever means are available through Presbytery.

4. *The Policy for Oversight of Chapels*

A. Definition—A chapel is a group of Christians working toward the development of an organized church, which serves as a mission outpost of an existing congregation.

B. Purposes—

   (1) A chapel is a means of carrying forth the mission of a local congregation, by reaching persons who would not ordinarily be reached by the ongoing ministry of that congregation.

   (2) A chapel exists to serve a community which would not otherwise be exposed to a Presbyterian witness.

   (3) The primary goal of any chapel is to work toward the establishment of a new congregation.

C. Guidelines for Oversight of Chapels by the Local Congregation

   (1) The chapel should be represented on the local church Session.

   (2) The local church Session is responsible for general oversight and support of the Chapel.

   (3) The local church Session is responsible to provide for supply pastors for worship, and regular observance of the Sacraments.

   (4) The local church Session should receive at least an annual report on the state of the Chapel.

D. Relationship of Chapels to Presbytery

   (1) The Subcommittee on Small Church Development should keep an up-to-date file on each chapel.

   (2) The subcommittee recommends to each Area Council that Chapels be given representation at Area meetings.

   (3) The Area Shepherds will be responsible to maintain ongoing contact with each chapel.

(4) The subcommittee recommends that each church Session submit an annual report to the subcommittee on the state of its chapels.

5. *The Policy of Expectations for Shared Ministry Pastors*

The Subcommittee on Small Church Development has the responsibility for oversight of all shared ministry congregations and pastors. We are concerned that each congregation have the type of pastoral leadership that will help it develop a more vital mission and program. To that end, the subcommittee shares the following minimum expectations for each shared ministry pastor.

    A. That first priority be given to the ongoing pastoral oversight of the congregation.

    B. That leadership be given in the development of program that will reflect a unique and needed ministry in the local congregation.

    C. That wherever possible the pastor give leadership in the local community as a whole.

    D. That the pastor be committed to working ecumenically whenever possible.

    E. That the pastor be committed to helping the congregation develop a sense of connectionalism, and fulfill its responsibilities to the various church judicatories.

6. *The Policy of Criteria for Recommending Financial Assistance to Shared Ministry Pastors*

The Subcommittee on Small Church Development will be guided by the following criteria when making recommendations for financial assistance for pastoral support to shared ministry churches. This is a set of general criteria and many specific considerations will be taken into account when evaluating whether a congregation meets the criteria. A church will be considered for financial assistance only if it meets at least one of the stated criteria.

    A. The continuation of the congregation is essential to the life and health of the local community.

    B. The congregation and the community offer potential for the development or continuation of some needed, unique ministry, which can best be carried out by that church.

    C. The congregation exhibits a high potential for growth and the development of ministry.

Other factors that will be taken into consideration when determining the need for financial assistance for pastoral support are as follows:

159

A. The leadership potential of the congregation.
B. The relationship of the congregation to Presbytery, and especially its openness and willingness to plan in cooperation with Presbytery.
C. The level of stewardship commitment of the members of the congregation.
D. The Mission Goals of the congregation.
E. The overall program of the church.

V. PROGRAMS FOR SMALL CHURCHES AND PASTORS

1. *The Area Shepherd Program*

One Area Shepherd will normally serve each of the six Areas of the Presbytery of Greenbrier. The Area Shepherds will fulfill the following responsibilities for Presbytery.

A. Coordinate the ministry of the small churches in each Area.
B. Communicate on a regular basis with the small churches and small church pastors in the Area.
C. Coordinate the evaluation-goal-setting process for shared ministry congregations in the Area.
D. Develop an ongoing relationship with the pastorless small churches and assist them in planning and developing effective ministry.
E. Be attached to the Division of Pastoral Care and report at regular intervals to the Division on the status of the small churches in the Area. The Area Shepherds shall be responsible to the special Presbyter who is assigned responsibility for coordinating the Area Shepherd network.

All expenses such as travel, phone bills, lodging, etc., that relate to Presbytery responsibilities will be paid by Presbytery.

F. New pastors in the Presbytery can be appointed to this responsibility only after a satisfactory orientation period on the field.

2. *The Program for Cooperative Parish Development*

The Subcommittee on Small Church Development affirms and encourages a program of cooperative parish development as one important means of enhancing the ministry of our small churches. A cooperative parish may be defined as two or more congregations cooperatively organizing around several agreed upon areas of mission in order to enhance the ministry of the participating churches.

As an initial phase in facilitating the development of cooperative parishes within the Presbytery of Greenbrier, we adopt the following policy:

160

A. To study and determine which geographic areas of the Presbytery might afford opportunities for cooperative parish development.

B. To begin discussions with other denominations that might lead toward ecumenical cooperative parish development.

C. To interpret the concept of the cooperative parish to local churches and to encourage them to consider such an option.

3. *The Program for Planning and Evaluation*

The Subcommittee on Small Church Development encourages all small churches and especially all shared ministry congregations to consider utilizing a comprehensive evaluation and process offered by the Presbytery. Part of this planning process includes a projection of financial needs over a four to five year period. A team of two persons from the Division of Pastoral Care will lead this planning process with each church that requests it.

Steps in the Process:

A. Gathering Information—A two-hour meeting with members of the entire congregation for the purpose of gathering complete data on the past, present, and future of the church and the community.

B. Goal Setting—A three-hour meeting with members of the congregation for the purpose of sharing hopes and concerns, and then writing goals and objectives based upon this information.

C. Expectations and Commitments—A planning meeting with the pastor, Session members, and other church officers to clarify expectations and responsibilities. Following this meeting members of the congregation will be asked to commit themselves to specific work groups to carry out the objectives.

D. Projecting Financial Needs—On the basis of the plans that have been worked out, the congregation's financial needs will be studied by the Session/officers.

4. *The Program of New Pastor Orientation*

The Subcommittee on Small Church Development recognizes the importance of orienting small church pastors to the unique nature and character of our small churches, and of offering practical helps for ministry in our area. Toward that end a series of five seminars will be offered each year. The seminars are as follows:

A. *CAM Orientation Conference*—A 3-day orientation seminar sponsored by CAM as a general orientation to ministry in Appalachia. This will normally be held in October and November.

161

B. *Introduction to Ministry in West Virginia.*—A one-day seminar held in January which will cover the following topics:
   1. General Introduction to West Virginia
   2. Historical Overview of West Virginia and the Presbyterian Church in W.Va.
   3. Cultural Characteristics of Rural West Virginians
   4. Sociological Overview of Community Structure and the Function of Religion in Community
   5. The Unique Religious Ethos of West Virginia.
   6. The Nature and Character of the Small Church
   7. Working with the Local Church
C. *Analytical Tools for Ministry*—A one-day seminar held in March which will cover the following topics:
   1. Analyzing and understanding the local community
   2. Analyzing and understanding the local church
   3. Analyzing personal strengths and weaknesses (including personal finances and personal life-style)
   4. Introduction to the Presbytery Structure and Philosophy
D. *Doing Theology*—A one-day seminar held in May that will deal with the following topics:
   1. The Theological Mindset of Rural West Virginians
   2. The Theological Task in the Local Church
   3. Assessing issues from the Christian perspective (land and land use, poverty and wealth in West Virginia, politics and government)
E. *Practical Aspects of Ministry*—A one-day seminar held in September dealing with the following topics:
   1. Planning and Program Development
   2. Working with the Church Session
   3. Leadership Development
   4. Factors in Church Growth
   5. Cooperative Ministry

Each one-day seminar will be held from 10:00 a.m. to 5:00 p.m. The format will include practical input from pastors who have had positive experience working with churches in West Virginia. A major emphasis will include sharing questions, ideas, and experiences by the participants.

5. *The Program of Peer/Colleague Support Groups*

Under the direction of the Special Presbyter for Counseling, peer support groups will be established in each of the Areas of the Presbytery of Greenbrier. Each group will seek to become a supportive community of ministers. The participants will meet together regularly to

162

seek strength and support for individual needs unique to the peer group; and to give strength and support to each other in dealing with some of the special demands unique to the peer group.

To achieve the goals of a support group, participants will become a community in covenant with one another in understanding and acceptance; sharing and caring. The groups will seek to develop relationships and understandings through sharing with one another in the following areas:

A. *Fellowship*—The groups will seek to offer the opportunity for participants to enjoy the friendship and fellowship of one another.

B. *Worship*—The groups will seek to provide a context for spiritual enrichment for the participants and an opportunity for expressions of their mutual faith and Christian commitment, through worship together.

C. *Professional Development*—The groups will provide a context for professional development and study through:
   1. Presenting position papers, sermons, or theses for study
   2. Sharing what has been tried in the practical context of the local church.
   3. Discussing issues in the world and larger society
   4. Using outside speakers or discussion leaders for dialogue in specific areas of concern to the group

D. *Peer/Colleague Support*—The groups will offer an opportunity for sharing and caring for one another through seeking to:
   1. Become a creative cadre of peers in the Christian faith
   2. Understand one another from a deeper level
   3. Know one another from different perspectives
   4. Encourage one another to reach out further
   5. Affirm the positive values of their work

Participation will be strictly voluntary. Each participant will assume personal responsibility for participation; free to say "yes" or "no" in any situation. The confidentiality of the group will be explicit. Group format and rules will be decided by each group.

CHAPTER THIRTEEN

Becoming a Community Based Congregation

The final stage in the revitalization process of the small church is the stage of becoming a community based congregation. As has been stated previously, the aim of revitalization is not to create smaller versions of large congregations. The aim of revitalization is to enable small churches to envision and accept that unique ministry of creating, undergirding and supporting community.

We live in a highly depersonalized society today. There is a growing need for groups and institutions to become communities where people can discover themselves in relationship to other human beings. Persons in our society need places where they can learn to care for and be cared for by other people. I believe it to be the unique nature and mission of the small church to create and undergird community for people today.

In that connection we need to return to our earlier definition of community as stated in chapter six. Community is a group of persons, living in relationship with one another, who act in concert to meet their mutual needs. And in this connection we are speaking of a particular type of community, i.e., a Christian community. The center of community for those in the church is always Jesus Christ. It is the common faith commitment in Jesus Christ that creates and holds community together.

This concept of community really brings to mind the Pauline definition of the church as the body of Christ. Paul's definition of the church as Christ's body is first of all a relational definition. It assumes an interdependence of care and support, in order for the body to be healthy. Secondly, it is a functional definition. It assumes that the body exists to perform the ministry of Jesus Christ in the world. The body is to be and to do, and its connecting link for support and strength is Christ himself.

The presupposition of this book has been that the small church is uniquely equipped to help create and support this kind of community. And the process of revitalization is aimed at enabling this to happen.

Each stage of the revitalization process enables a small church to move in the direction of becoming a Christian community. The stage of reaffirmation enables the members of the church to reaffirm the worth of their small size. It enables them to reaffirm their basic caring functions of one another. It enables them to reaffirm how their small church has undergirded community in the past. It enables them to affirm that they have a special reason for being.

The second stage of the process, the stage of initial victories enables the laity of a small church to experience success. It enables them to see that their strength lies not just in the past, but also in the present. It enables them to affirm their ability to become a vital and relevant institution today.

The third stage of discovering a new identity is the stage in which the people of a small church can more clearly begin to envision what it would mean to be a community based congregation today. It enables them to discover the biblical concept of Christian community and to understand how that relates to the present day. It enables them to see that their mission and purpose is not just to themselves, but to others who are not part of their group. It stirs the need to begin relating to the people and institutions about them.

During the fourth stage, the small church becomes equipped to assess its needs and develop ways of becoming a stronger congregation. It is during this phase that the small church actually begins to develop plans for reaching out into the local area in a more effective way.

The final stage is the point at which the small church actually begins the process of reaching out beyond itself. This is the stage when the small church begins its community based ministry, as a revitalized organism.

It needs to be stressed that these five stages are not totally distinct. There are points at which they overlap and coalesce. But each is an essential part of the revitalization process.

A caution also needs to be added at this point with regard to a small church creating and undergirding community. A single small church must never envision itself as the totality of community. This has been one of the basic problems of the small church in the past. They have been exclusive, making it most difficult for new people to become part of the group.

To become a Christian community a small church must be inclusive, always seeking new ways of bringing others into the community of faith, and reaching out to penetrate the larger community around it.

It was previously stated in chapter six that the small church could serve as the foundation of community in at least three ways. First is spiritually. Second is relationally in terms of personal support. And third is in conjunction with the church building itself becoming a center for community activity.

Certainly each is a valid function for any small church.

The need for being the spiritual leaven for society is essential. It is at this point that the church should be challenging some of the materialistic values of modern society. The small church by its very nature questions the values of bigness, production, and acquisition of wealth, as the purposes of human existence. These values need to be questioned even more openly and aggressively. The small church is in a position to reaffirm basic spiritual values and belief as being truly central to human existence. And that is the beginning of creating community.

The relational nature of the small church is its most appealing characteristic. Part of its mission when it becomes a community based congregation, is to extend those natural caring functions to others outside the church. This is especially true of the poor and dispossessed. It is not just the mission of the church to have programs to feed and clothe the poor. It is even more essential to begin relating to the poor as persons, and offer the emotional and spiritual support that they so often seek.

And any small church can certainly become a center for activity. The building itself can become central to community activities. But more important the small church needs to be involved in assessing local needs and helping to initiate and support programs to meet those needs. In all these ways the small church is uniquely equipped to become the foundation of community.

Perhaps the presupposition of the small church becoming the foundation for community sounds idealistic. Certainly this process of revitalization is a long and difficult one. And there is no assurance that any small church that goes through a planned process of revitalization will become a community based church.

The fact is that the small church faces many problems and difficulties. Small churches all over this nation have endured a long and difficult history of misunderstanding and neglect. The needs of these small churches and the solutions that will lead toward revitalization are both complex and difficult.

And yet, I am generally optimistic about the future of the small church. I'm optimistic because some of the things that are being tried seem to be working. I'm optimistic because of the innate resiliency and indigenous strength that have epitomized small churches in the past. I'm optimistic because of the kind of people and the quality of human relationships that so often typify small churches. But most of all I am optimistic because of God's continuing presence with these small churches, and the unique mission that He has bestowed upon them.

However, wishful thinking is not enough. The revitalization of small churches that suffer from the survival syndrome is going to demand careful planning on the part of denominations. A broad scoped, long range strategy must be developed. The purpose of this book has been a detail some of the concepts that need to be incorporated in such a strategy.

The starting point for developing comprehensive strategies for the revitalization of small churches is to understand their unique character. By building upon that unique nature it is possible that many small churches could become genuine Christian communities, undergirding and supporting community life in general.

We therefore must begin with an image of what could be. We must fully understand the need for the rediscovery of community in our depersonalized, bureaucratized world. We must begin to envision community as a dynamic relationally based group of persons, living and working together, with their lives centered on a spiritual base. And then we need to understand the basic nature of the small church as existing to undergird and create this kind of community.

The need is to enable small churches to move beyond survival toward this unique mission. The need is for small church pastors to rediscover their identity and life in the context of church and community. The need is for denominational judicatories to undergo some rather basic changes in philosophy and structure that will enable them to support the reemergence of the small church as the foundation of community. But the most pressing need is to move beyond theoretical conceptualizations toward practical changes.

Most of all we need to remain open to the leading of God's spirit in this venture. Unless we are guided by God's spirit we can never help the small church to move beyond survival to creative mission.

Bibliography

Buber, Martin. *Paths in Utopia.* Translated by R. F. C. Hull. Beacon Press, 1970.

Caudill, Harry M. *Night Comes to the Cumberlands.* Boston: Little Brown and Company, 1961.

Dudley, Carl S. *Making The Small Church Effective.* Nashville: Abingdon Press, 1978.

Eliade, Mirea. *The Sacred and the Profane.* (Translated Willard R. Trask) New York: Harper and Row, 1961.

Kaufman, Harold F. "Toward an Interactional Conception of Community," *Perspectives of the American Community.* Edited by Roland Warren. Chicago: Rand McNally, 1973.

Lambert, Oscar D. *Stephen B. Elkins.* Pittsburgh: University of Pittsburgh Press, 1953.

Latourette, Kenneth Scott. *A History of Christianity.* New York: Harper and Brothers, 1953.

Lee, Howard. *Bloodletting in Appalachia.* Parsons, W.Va.: McClain Printing Company, 1964.

Littell, Franklin Hamlin. *From State Church to Pluralism.* Garden City, N.Y.: Doubleday and Company, Inc., 1962.

Lynd, Robert S., and Lynd, Helen Merrell. *Middletown.* New York: Harcourt, Brace and World, Inc., 1956.

Morgan, Arthur E. *The Small Community.* New York: Harper and Brothers, 1942.

Morris, Homer Lawrence. *The Plight of the Bituminous Coal Miner.* Philadelphia: University of Pennsylvania Press, 1934.

Nisbet, Robert A. *The Sociological Tradition.* New York: Basic Books, Inc., 1966.

Pope, Liston. *Mill Hands and Preachers.* New Haven: Yale University Press, 1967.

Rich, Mark. *Some Churches in Coal Mining Communities of West Virginia.* New York: West Virginia Council of Churches, 1951.

Sandeen, Ernest R. *The Roots of Fundamentalism.* Chicago: The University of Chicago Press, 1970.

Smith, H. Shelton, Handy, Robert T., and Lectcher, Lefferts H. *American Christianity, An Historical Interpretation with Representative Documents.* Vols. 1 and 2. New York: Charles Scribner's Sons, 1960.

Summers, Festus P. *Johnson Newton Camden: A Study in Individualism.* New York: G. P. Putnam's Sons, 1937.

Tams, Jr. *The Smokeless Coalfields of West Virginia.* Parsons: McClain Printing Company, 1963.

Wallace, Robert. "The Rugged Basis of American Protestantism," *Life Magazine.* Chicago: Time-Life Publications, December 16, 1967.

Worley, Robert C. *Change in the Church: A Source of Hope.* Philadelphia: The Westminster Press, 1974.